EVERY KNEE
SHALL BOW

EVERY KNEE
SHALL BOW

An Invitation and a Warning from the Sovereign God of the Universe to All Political Leaders of Earth

R. Alan Smith

WINGS OF EAGLES PRESS ™

Isaiah 40:31

San Diego, California

2015

First Printing: October 2014

ISBN 978-0692287101

Library of Congress Control Number: 2014951836
Wings of Eagles Press, San Diego, California

Unless otherwise indicated, Bible quotations are from the HOLY BIBLE, NEW INTERNATIONAL VERSION. Copyright © 1973, 1978, 1984 by International Bible Society. Used by permission of Zondervan. All rights reserved.

Scripture quotations marked (TLB) are from *The Living Bible* © 1971 by Tyndale House Foundation. Used by permission of Tyndale House Publishers Inc., Carol Stream, Illinois 60188. All rights reserved.

Scripture quotations marked (MSG) are from *The Message*. Copyright © 1993, 1994, 1995, 1996, 2000, 2001, 2002. Used by permission of NavPress Publishing Group.

Quantity Discounts: Special discounts may be available on quantity purchases by churches, ministries, associations, corporations, and individuals. For details, contact discounts@wingsofeaglespress.net.

Publisher Website: www.wingsofeaglespress.net

Printed By: CreateSpace, An Amazon Company

eStore Address: www.CreateSpace.com/4370626

Available in print and as an eBook from Amazon.com, CreateSpace.com, and other retail outlets.

DEDICATION

To my father, a man of few words, who modelled for me in many actions how to be a rock-steady man of faith, a reliable and loving parent, a trustworthy and caring husband, and a dependable shepherd-protector of his family.

To political leaders at every level, in every nation:

- Who seek to serve God by serving His People;
- Who seek to serve Him above all other interests, including their own self-interest;
- Who, in doing so, resolve to be virtuous and effective political leaders, worthy of being called *political leaders* rather than mere *politicians*.

To the more than seven billion citizens of earth, created in the image of God, who deserve to be served by virtuous and effective political leaders.

CONTENTS

Preface
Buckle Up!   11

Chapter 1
Speak! Write!   13

Chapter 2
The Sorry State of Political Leadership Around the World   23

Chapter 3
Politics As Sacred Vocation   31

Chapter 4
The Sovereignty of God   41

Chapter 5
Government from the Perspective of the Sovereign God   47

Chapter 6
The Sovereign God's Invitation to ALL Political Leaders   59

Chapter 7
The Sovereign God's Warning to ALL Political Leaders   65

Chapter 8
If a Political Leader Doesn't Believe The Message   71

Chapter 9
A Final Message To Political Leaders: "A Time to Choose"   79

Chapter 10
A Message to the Nations: "Come Home!"   89

Afterword
How You Can Help Release God's Power   97

About the Author   105

* * * * * * * * * *

He brings princes to naught
*   and reduces the rulers of this world to*
*   nothing.*
No sooner are they planted,
*   no sooner are they sown,*
*   no sooner do they take root in the ground,*
than he blows on them and they wither,
*   and a whirlwind sweeps them away like chaff.*

"To whom will you compare me?
*   Or who is my equal?" says the Holy One.*[1]

* * * * * * * * * *

It is written:

"'As surely as I live,' says the Lord,
*   'every knee will bow before me;*
*   every tongue will acknowledge God.'"*[2]

* * * * * * * * * *

---

[1] Isaiah 40:23-25

[2] Romans 14:11

* * * * * * * * * *

*The greatest question of our time is not
communism vs. individualism, not Europe vs.
America, not even the East vs. the West; it is
whether men can bear to live without God.* [3]

* * * * * * * * * *

*I come before you as a witness: a witness to
human dignity, a witness to hope, a witness to
the conviction that the destiny of all nations lies
in the hands of a merciful Providence.* [4]

* * * * * * * * * *

*I've read the last page of the Bible.
It's all going to turn out all right.* [5]

* * * * * * * * * *

---

[3] Will Durant, *On the Meaning of Life* (New York: Ray Long & Richard R. Smith, Inc., 1932) 23

[4] Address of His Holiness Pope John Paul II to the Fiftieth General Assembly of the United Nations Organization, New York, October 5, 1995

[5] Rev. Billy Graham

PREFACE

BUCKLE UP!

*Let us speak of these [roles of the church] as
"priestly" and "prophetic." The priestly will
normally be celebrative, affirmative, culture-
building. The prophetic will tend to be
dialectical about civil religion, but with a
predisposition toward the judgmental. The two
are translations of Joseph Pulitzer's definition
of the compleat journalist or, in my application,
of the fulfilled religionist: one comforts the
afflicted; the other afflicts the comfortable.* [6]

This is *not* the book I planned to write. Frankly, it's *not* the book I wanted to write. But it IS the book I was meant to write.

If left to my own devices, my original concept was simple:

- Make a thoughtful contribution to the public discourse on the current state of political affairs in the Western world, viewed from a Christian perspective.

- Employ quotes from learned people throughout history from the fields of politics, religion and philosophy in order to demonstrate how well-read I am – not for the purpose of showing off, mind you,

---

[6] Martin Marty, *Religion and Republic: The American Circumstance* (Beacon Press, MA, First Edition, 1987), p. 82

but to demonstrate that I *must* know what I'm talking about.

- Engage in a careful examination of different political theories and systems through the ages and how they might fit, or not fit, a Christian worldview.
- Stir up a lively conversation on what makes for effective government and political leadership of which God might look with favor.
- Be socially acceptable, which means no "rocking the boat" and, by all means, playing it safe.

The Sovereign God of the Universe had a different idea. He would have none of it! While He gives me some space of my own to write, He has figuratively, if not literally, "grabbed the microphone" because He has a lot on His Mind with regard to the subject of government and political leadership. And He wants to speak directly (and frankly) to ALL political leaders ALL around the world.

Who am I to say no to Him?

The afflicted (the governed) are about to be comforted. And the comfortable (political leaders) are about to be afflicted.

The Spirit of the Lord is upon me.

R. Alan Smith
September 1, 2014

P.S. Buckle up!

CHAPTER 1

SPEAK! WRITE!

"The two most important days in your life are the day you are born and the day you find out why." [7]

[W]hat a nation needs more than anything else is not a Christian ruler in the palace, but a Christian prophet within earshot. [8]

"You must go to everyone I send you to and say whatever I command you." [9]

I'm 66 years old. Over the past 40 years, I've had a diverse career: lawyer, political professional, nonprofit association executive, governmental affairs professional, strategic advisor, executive coach, and university professor.

Becoming a prophet was never on my "List Of Things To Do When I Grow Up." Yet it appears to have been on God's "List Of Things For Alan To Do" since long before I was born. He tells me that my entire life has been in preparation for this moment, and for all the moments that are to come.

I write from three perspectives: a life of faith, a life as a political insider, and as one who has received a prophetic

---

[7] Mark Twain

[8] Kenneth Kaunda, President of Zambia (1964 to 1991)

[9] Jeremiah 1:7

calling. This is the only chapter about me. I only tell it to you because:

- If you don't know who has delivered the message, and WHO is the sender, then why should you pay attention?
- If you don't know who has brought the invitation, and WHO has issued it, then why should you respond?
- If you don't know who has given the warning, and WHO has authorized it, then why should you consider yourself warned?

While I may agree with all that is said here, nothing is offered as my opinion. Nothing is offered as one point of view to be considered among a multitude of equally valid points of view.

What IS offered here is a direct message from the Sovereign God of the Universe. Whether you're a political leader or one of the governed, you ignore it at your peril.

PERSPECTIVE #1: A LIFE OF FAITH

I haven't lived a charmed life, a life unaffected by dangers and difficulties. But I have lived a blessed life.

Of the 24,134 days that I've been alive, I can't remember a single day when the Sovereign God of the Universe wasn't present and actively involved in my life.

He has been My Shepherd [10] in every sense of the word, especially on the darkest of my days, of which there have been many:

- When I fell, He picked me up, dusted me off, and stood me upright again.
- When I was too weak to go on, He carried me upon His Shoulders until I regained my strength.

---

[10] Psalm 23

- When I was at Death's Door, He laid claim to my life and rescued me.
- When I was wounded, He put salve on my wounds, bound them up, and nursed me back to health.
- When I strayed from His watchful eye, He came looking for me until He found me and brought me back to safety.

PERSPECTIVE #2: A LIFE AS A POLITICAL INSIDER

I'm not an ill-informed, cranky critic standing comfortably on the sidelines pointing my finger at those inside the political arena. I AM a political insider.

For more than forty years I've been a political warrior navigating the treacherous seas where law, business, politics, government, media, and public opinion converge.

Those who know me best think I eat, breathe and dream politics. Perhaps I do, though my interests are far more encompassing.

I've always been fascinated by the political process:

- I was active in student government in high school and college.
- I've been a senior advisor, strategist and political operative on numerous political campaigns.
- I've built and orchestrated demanding, complex, fast-moving political operations that would overwhelm most political and non-political people I know.
- I've been a public policy advocate on a wide range of issues at national, state and local levels.
- I've taught political science and organizational politics at a Christian university.
- The walls of my home are lined with row-upon-row of books on history and politics.

I've even had my own political dreams and aspirations: City Councilman, Mayor, State Legislator, Member of the United States Congress, United States Senator. I've charted my political course and I've acquired all the skills and experience needed to be successful at it.

But every time I charted my own course for political office, the Sovereign God seemed to shift the winds ever so slightly, blowing me off course, though never onto the rocks.

The Divine Course Corrections in my life have always felt purposeful, even if I couldn't always discern their purpose.

With the passage of too much time to launch a meaningful political career of my own, I concluded that my destiny was to devote my remaining productive years to developing effective and virtuous political leaders around the world. So I further enhanced my knowledge and skills, acquiring the skills and credentials of an executive coach, charting a course to becoming a recognized international leader in the field.

That may yet happen, but the Sovereign God had one more, very major, course correction for me. This may be my final destination, the task for which He has been preparing me for my entire life.

It appears that He *never* intended for me to become a political leader myself. But He *did* want me to have an intimate acquaintance with life in the political arena.

PERSPECTIVE #3: A PROPHETIC CALLING

The Sovereign God has spoken to me intermittently through the years, almost always at 3:00 AM. I'm certain that's because at 3:00 AM I'm too tired to argue or question, and I'm the most willing to listen.

Several years ago, the Sovereign God woke me up at 3:00 AM and here is EXACTLY what He said to me:

Before you were born,
Before the Foundation of the World,
I appointed you to be a prophet to the nations,
To come forward at this exact moment in history
To proclaim My Word to ALL political leaders of
earth.

The message was as startling to me then as it may be to you now. It echoed the prophetic call of Jeremiah:

Before I formed you in the womb I knew you,
before you were born I set you apart;
I appointed you as a prophet to the nations. [11]

I tried to dismiss the experience as the product of an overactive imagination coupled with reading the Bible at bedtime. While an admirer of Jeremiah, Isaiah, Ezekiel, Daniel, and other Old Testament Prophets, I harbored no ambitions or aspirations to follow in their footsteps. But the Sovereign God visited me night after night, precisely at 3:00 AM, and gave me the identical message until I was finally convicted of its authenticity.

I began to read everything I could get my hands on to help me understand what it means to be a prophet to the nations. But I kept the experience to myself. And, I thought, so long as no one else knew – except the Sovereign God, of course – I wouldn't have to do anything about it … at least until I was ready to take action.

Then one evening, perhaps six months later, a trusted friend who'd been somewhat of a spiritual mentor to me unexpectedly called. We hadn't spoken in quite some time, and I certainly hadn't written, emailed, or otherwise communicated to her anything about my 3:00 AM wake-up calls … lest she insist on knowing what I intended to do about

---

[11] Jeremiah 1:5

it.

To the best of my recollection here's what my friend said to me, not yet knowing what I already knew:

> *Alan, on the day we first met more than ten years ago, the LORD sent me to meet you. He showed me something on that day and told me to keep it to myself until He instructed me otherwise. Well, He has now told me to tell you what I saw.*
>
> *Alan, as I saw you walking down the hall toward me, the LORD said to me, "Behold, a prophet to the nations!"*

Confirmation from one of the people I trust the most! It was a validation of the message I had received so that I wouldn't think, or couldn't say, I'd misheard or misunderstood Him. Now there was no escaping or avoiding the call.

The Sovereign God then coaxed me over a period of months to tell several other friends whom I trust with my life, my reputation, and my secrets – which are few. None of them laughed or questioned. Each immediately embraced the idea, both of the message and my appointment as the messenger. And each has relentlessly inquired, undoubtedly at the prodding of the Sovereign God: *"what are you doing about it?"* and (once they knew about this book) *"when will your book be finished?"*

Over the months that followed I continued to try to understand exactly what it was that He wanted me to do. The answer over and over, and always at 3:00 AM, consisted of only two words: *"Speak! Write!"*

GENESIS OF THIS BOOK

And then a Catholic friend invited me to go with him to an Assemblies of God men's retreat where the following Bible verse was printed big and bold on the program cover for the final day's worship service:

"This is what the Lord, the God of Israel, says: 'Write in a book all the words I have spoken to you." [12]

I now knew what to do with *"Speak! Write!"* The Sovereign God had given me a mandate to write this book so that ALL political leaders of earth will know what He expects – no, what He demands – of them at this precise moment in history.

I'm compelled by the Sovereign God of the Universe to deliver His Message, to extend His Invitation, and to issue His Warning, to ALL political leaders of earth – not just to the political leaders of my own nation.

It's a responsibility I don't take lightly and for which I'd never volunteer. As I've protested to Him that I'm not up to the task, He has assured me that I know everything I need to know, and that I am everything I need to be in order for Him to be able to use me in this way.

He has also made clear that my job is not to persuade any political leader as to the authenticity of the message. That's something that political leaders will have to decide for themselves – though they ignore it at their peril. My three-part task is simply this: (1) to deliver His Message, (2) to extend His Invitation, and (3) to issue His Warning.

---

[12] Jeremiah 30:2

The matter is urgent:

> *One reason that tyranny has been so serious in the twentieth century is the lack of prophets among the nations. There have been no prophets challenging political rulers to obey God. Many rulers do not even know that they are required to serve God, or that he has put limits on their jurisdiction. God can only act against evil rulers, if he has a prophet to speak out his challenge and warn of his judgments (Amos 3:7)* [13]

WHY NOW? WHY IS A WARNING NEEDED?

Why now? Because the Sovereign God says it is time! The Day of Reckoning, or Day of Judgment, is upon us. And the coming of the Kingdom of God is imminent. Because we're living in times that are far more dangerous than we've ever known before and far more dangerous than we and our political leaders seem to comprehend.

Why a warning? Because the Sovereign God is a Just God, He won't execute on His Judgment until those who are to be judged have been warned of the charges against them. He stays His Hand until they have had an opportunity to turn away from the course of conduct which has incurred His Wrath. But once the warning has been given, if they don't repent and turn away from that course of conduct, He is then free to execute on His Judgment.

Unless you knew of my prophetic calling, you might not realize that you'd been warned by the Sovereign God's servant.

---

[13] Ron McKenzie, *Prophetic Ministry* (Kingwatch Books, Christchurch, New Zealand, 2012), p. 67

But now you do know. And here is the essence of what He has to say:

TO ALL POLITICAL LEADERS OF EARTH: THIS IS THE WORD OF THE SOVEREIGN GOD TO YOU

I am the Sovereign God of the Universe and I have anointed a Prophet to the Nations,

I have instructed him to write and speak.

My Message to you is now being delivered by him.

My Servant is now extending My Invitation to you to bow down before, and serve, Me.

My Servant is issuing My Warning as to what will happen to you if you fail to turn away from the course of conduct which has incurred My Wrath.

* * * * * * * * * *

If the message of this book can be summarized in a single sentence, it's this: *"Get your political house in order, or the Sovereign God of the Universe will do it for you!"*

Time is running out and the clock is ticking. You have been warned!

R. Alan Smith
September 1, 2014

CHAPTER 2

THE SORRY STATE OF POLITICAL LEADERSHIP AROUND THE WORLD

There is not a square inch in the whole domain of our human existence over which Christ, who is Sovereign over all, does not cry, "Mine!" [14]

But you are so foolish and so ignorant! Because you are in darkness, all the foundations of society are shaken to the core. [15]

TO ALL POLITICAL LEADERS OF EARTH: THIS IS THE WORD OF THE SOVEREIGN GOD TO YOU

Comes now the Sovereign and Almighty God of the Bible, the Creator and Sustainer of the Universe, who stands astride the arc of history, with one foot firmly planted at the beginning of time (the Creation) and the other firmly planted at the end of time (the Day of Judgment), to lay claim to the Public Square.

I created man (male and female) in My Own Image, as the Jewel of My Creation, as the Object of My Bounty and as the Focus of My Love. I declare My Lordship over every aspect of the affairs of man, including politics, economics, government, and international relations.

---

[14] Abraham Kuyper, Prime Minister of the Netherlands (1901-1905)

[15] Psalm 82:5 (TLB)

I have written the storyline of history. I bend history according to My Will, to serve My Purposes, and to further My Plan. I declare that the Day of Reckoning, also called the Day of Judgment, is at hand.

From the beginning of time, up to and including this very moment, I have put political leaders in power and removed them according to My Will, when it served My Purposes, and when it furthered My Plan. I declare that the authority of any and all political leaders to preside over the affairs of man is derivative – it comes directly and exclusively from Me.

I preside over the Kingdom of God, the arrival of which is imminent. I have examined your earthly kingdoms, nations and states. Despite your best efforts to devise utopian schemes, or to create perfect political systems, or to fashion ideal policy solutions, I find them to be weak imitations and vain imaginings of the Kingdom Which Is About to Come.

I am the Author, the Principal Actor, the Director, the Producer, and the Guiding Force in the entire story of human history, from start to finish. I declare that the theme and focus of that history is My Inexorable Plan for the Redemption of Man – it cannot and will not be stopped, changed or thwarted.

You live and breathe by My Grace. You occupy positions of political leadership by virtue of My Authority. I have examined the General State of Political Leadership Worldwide and I AM NOT PLEASED:

THE INDICTMENT

- *I find political leaders who are virtuous but ineffective, lacking the basic skills, intellectual discipline, and self-regulation essential to doing the work to which they have been called.*
- *I find political leaders who are effective but utterly lacking in the basic virtues required of one who*

wears the mantle of the Sovereign God's Authority.

- *I find political leaders who make fools of themselves and a mockery of their office by engaging in shameful and disreputable conduct.*
- *I find political leaders who cannot, or will not, harness their ambition for good, thus becoming slaves to their own ambition and passions.*
- *I find political leaders more interested in engaging in political theater than in getting anything of significance done.*
- *I find political leaders who are so ineffective or self-serving that the people whom they govern have lost faith in them as leaders.*
- *I find political leaders who are derelict in their duties, spinning their wheels, running in place, lacking a clear sense of direction or purpose, focused on the irrelevant, absorbed with advancing or protecting their own careers, obsessed by the pursuit of position and power for the sake of nothing more than their own self-preservation, self-advancement and self-glorification.*
- *I find political leaders who turn a blind eye to injustice and corruption, or worse, who engage in and encourage injustice and corruption.*
- *I find political leaders who love the game of politics more than they love Me, or the governed whom I have entrusted to their care.*
- *I find political leaders who are narcissistic and love their own reflected glory more than they love the reflection of the Living God seen in the faces of the men, women and children whom I have created and whom these political leaders are supposed to serve.*
- *I find political leaders who are more interested in using the powers and tools of government to benefit themselves and their wealthy and powerful*

friends, donors, and cronies, than in using those powers and tools to promote the welfare of the governed, especially the weak and the powerless.

- *I find political leaders who are in direct opposition to Me: authoritarians, oppressors, tyrants, and thugs who seek to force a yoke upon the necks of the men, women and children whom I have created, who I love, and to whose rescue I will shortly come.*

- *I find political leaders who create chaos and destabilize societies, economies, and governments to suit their own political, economic, and military ends.*

- *I am about to set the political house in order throughout the world, and I am fully able to do so. I will depose those political leaders who displease Me, and raise up others to replace them.*

As I have said it, so shall it be.

Amen

* * * * * * * * * *

Your attention is called to Psalm 82 in the Old Testament of the Bible. The Psalmist imagines the Sovereign God presiding over a great assembly of "the gods." The translators of the New International Version put "the gods" in quotations to suggest that as a result of their own hubris and sense of self-importance these earthly rulers consider themselves to be "gods" or at least equal to the Sovereign God.

One can imagine their smugness as they wait for the Sovereign God to speak to them. How very pleased He must be with them: their abilities, their achievements, and especially their status.

The words of the Sovereign God are brief, to the point, and blistering:

> *"How long will you defend the unjust*
> *and show partiality to the wicked?"* [16]

These are not the congratulatory words expected by the assembled "gods," but an indictment. They have now been knocked down a peg or two to the status of mere "earthly rulers," or, worse yet, "the accused." Before they can catch their collective breath, the Sovereign God continues with an admonition:

> *"Defend the weak and the fatherless;*
> *uphold the cause of the poor and the*
> *oppressed.*
> *Rescue the weak and the needy;*
> *deliver them from the hand of the wicked."* [17]

It's a stinging rebuke to these self-righteous rulers, casting a blinding beam of light on their wickedness. They've been derelict in their duty to protect the powerless against all who would oppress or exploit them.

Then the Sovereign God laments aloud the sorry state of these earthly rulers who have become self-important, self-styled "gods":

> *"The 'gods' know nothing,*
> *they understand nothing.*
> *They walk about in darkness;*
> *all the foundations of the earth are shaken."* [18]

---

[16] Psalm 82:2

[17] Psalm 82:3-4

[18] Psalm 82:5

These "know-it-alls," know nothing. They are the blind leading the blind. As the foundations of the earth are being shaken, these political leaders have abdicated their duties because they are too busy serving their own interests and/or the interests of their friends, patrons and cronies.

The Sovereign God's disappointment in, and despair over, them is evident. These esteemed earthly rulers, whom He has personally invested with great power and with His Own Authority, have failed His Children, and thus have failed Him.

> *"I said, 'You are "gods";*
> *you are all sons of the Most High.'*
> *But you will die like mere mortals;*
> *you will fall like every other ruler." [19]*

Where are the self-styled great and impactful leaders of history: Alexander the Great, Cyrus the Great, Darius the Great, Emperor Gaozu of Han, Julius Caesar, Caesar Augustus, Napoleon, Hitler, or Stalin? All dead.

Where is the Sovereign God? Still living and impacting history yesterday, today, and tomorrow.

Where are the self-styled great and impactful empires of history: The Roman Empire, the Mongol Empire, the Russian Empire, the Holy Roman Empire, the British Empire, the Napoleonic Empire, the Han Dynasty, the Byzantine Empire, the Persian Empire, the Umayyad Caliphate, the Ottoman Empire, the Third Reich, the Soviet Union? Dismantled. Destroyed. Turned to dust and ashes.

Where is the Kingdom of God? It's on its way and will be here sooner than you imagine. And when it arrives, it will sweep away ALL earthly kingdoms, all self-styled empires; while the Kingdom of God will endure forever.

---

[19] Psalm 82:6-7

The Psalmist closes with this plea:

Rise up, O God, judge the earth,
for all the nations are your inheritance. [20]

The Sovereign God now summons ALL political leaders of the present age to gather for another great assembly:

- From every nation.
- From every system on the political spectrum: from the most democratic to the most authoritarian.
- From every branch of government: executive, legislative, and judicial.
- Christian believers of every stripe: Catholic, Eastern Orthodox, Anglican, Episcopalian, Evangelical, Protestant, Latter Day Saint, and all others.
- Jews: Orthodox, Conservative, Reformed, and secular.
- Muslims: Shi'ite and Sunni.
- Buddhist, Hindu, and all other religions.
- The undecided Agnostics and the unbelieving Atheists.

Attendance at this assembly is not optional. The Sovereign God calls you forward one by one to give an account of your own stewardship as a political leader. You have been invested with great power and with the Sovereign God's Own Authority. He wants to hear you give an account of how you think you've been doing. But know this: He already knows.

He calls you by name. He knows who you are. He knows everything about you, including those things you thought were secret. He reads your heart and mind. Nothing is hidden from Him.

---

[20] Psalm 82:8

And lest you find comfort that there are others "worse" than you, do not be comforted. For the Sovereign God does not measure you in comparison to other political leaders. He will judge you on your own merits, against His Own Standards, and based upon what He has called you to do for Him and for His Children.

What will **YOU** say to Him?

What will **HE** say to you?

* * * * * * * * * *

May the Sovereign God have mercy on you as you stand before Him.

CHAPTER 3

POLITICS AS SACRED VOCATION

I ask God to give us more politicians capable of sincere and effective dialogue aimed at healing the deepest roots – and not simply the appearances – of the evils of our world! Politics, though often denigrated, remains a lofty vocation and one of the highest forms of charity, inasmuch as it seeks the common good... I beg the Lord to grant us more politicians genuinely disturbed by the state of society, the people, the lives, of the poor! [21]

... a great politician's career remorselessly sucks everything into its vortex – including his family and even his dog. [22]

IN THE POLITICAL ARENA

Every morning men and women around the world leave the relative peace and comfort of their beds to climb into the ego-bruising, often brutish, all-consuming, sometimes dehumanizing, always rough-and-tumble arena where the drama of politics is played out.

---

[21] Pope Francis, *The Joy of the Gospel: Evangelii Gaudium* (United States Conference of Catholic Bishops, 2013), p. 103

[22] James MacGregor Burns, *Roosevelt: The Lion and the Fox (1882-1940)* (Harcourt, Brace & World, New York, 1956), p. ix

Driven by a variety of motivations, every day these men and women risk their names, their reputations, their integrity, their egos, and sometimes their fortunes, to participate in the public life of their villages, cities, regions, states, provinces, and nations.

Their sacrifices are far greater than the casual observer on the sidelines of the public arena can ever grasp. Sometimes their sacrifices are even greater than they, or their families, realize – until it is too late.

All day, every day, political leaders have to make dozens, if not hundreds, of choices between what's right and what's wrong. The rightness or wrongness of a choice is sometimes obvious (e.g. to take a bribe or not); more often rightness or wrongness is in the eye of the beholder (e.g. will this policy truly help the poor, or will it inadvertently hurt them?) Rarely are political decisions presented in neatly-wrapped black or white packages, tied up with pretty bows. More often they come in untidy packages wrapped in various shades of gray butcher paper, and the political leader is forced to choose between two or more less-than-perfect policy alternatives. The sheer number of daily ethical decisions would exhaust, if not overwhelm, most of us.

All day, every day, political leaders are buffeted by forces beyond their control. Several years after his retirement as the 33rd President of the United States (1945-1952), Harry S. Truman wrote that

> *Within the first few months, I discovered that being a President is like riding a tiger. A man has to keep on riding or be swallowed.* [23]

Regardless of the political office held, the political life is never a leisurely stroll in the park. More often than not it's a hold-on-for-your-life ride through the political jungle on the

---

[23] Harry S Truman Quoted in the *New York Times*, 28 Dec 1984

back of a tiger which is more than willing to eat you if you lose your grip, all while hundreds of people (media, supporters, opponents, interest groups, financial backers, colleagues, and party leaders) are throwing rocks and hurling spears at you, or at each other, and poking sticks at the tiger on which you're riding. It's never easy, and it's far from glamorous.

WHY DO THEY DO IT?

There are political leaders who are driven to enter the political arena by a sincere desire to change the world – whatever that may mean to them. Perhaps changing the world into something that has never before been seen, an as-yet-unfulfilled potential. Perhaps restoring the world to some former state perceived by them to have been better than now. They may want to change the entire world, or their goal may be more modest: changing the villages, cities, regions, states, provinces, or nations in which they live.

There are political leaders who don't necessarily want to change the world, but they do want to be engaged in some great and noble cause. They view participation in the political process as just such a cause. They see a need in the political arena. They believe they have the requisite skills, and that they have something to contribute. So they step forward to offer all that they have to give.

But far too many political leaders enter the political arena for less inspiring motives: to satisfy some ego need. They may want the stimulation, the adrenaline-rush that political combat can provide seven days a week, twenty-four hours a day. They may think that being in the political spotlight will make them not just feel important, but actually BE important. They may view a political life as way of getting approval, attention, even adulation – either from their fellow citizens or perhaps from their families. They may find gratification, meaning, and self-worth in making weighty decisions, in dispensing favors, in wheeling-and-dealing, in rubbing shoulders with the economic and political elite, in joining the ranks of the economic and political elite, in being at the very center of gravity of momentous decisions and events. Such political leaders are weaker than they think because their sense of self-worth is built on a shaky foundation, and they seek validation in a very harsh and unfriendly environment. As President Truman is reputed to have colorfully said, "If you want a friend in Washington, get a dog." The same could be said in any national, state, or provincial capital, or at any city or village hall.

Then there are those who enter the political arena for the basest of all motives: what philosopher and cultural critic Friedrich Nietzsche described as *"the will to power"* [24] – the desire to inflict one's will on others, to bring others under one's control and domination by any means necessary, and at any cost. The craving for power of these political leaders is limitless. They never have enough power because there are always more subjects to conquer, and a steady supply of power is needed to keep under subjugation those already under their control and domination.

The political arena is populated by a wide range of characters, many of them good men and women, most with the best of intentions, but there are far too many whose path you would never want your children to cross. Politics is a strange business. It's not for the faint of heart. But it's an important business.

The chief reason why the worldwide state of political leadership is in such a sorry state is that for too many of the players, politics has become a secular profession, a high-stakes game, rather than the sacred vocation intended by the Sovereign God.

As strange as it may sound in this so-called "enlightened" Age of Modernity or Postmodernity, the political life is a sacred vocation in a general sense, and in

---

[24] Friedrich Nietzsche, *The Will to Power* (Random House, 1968)

one very specific sense.

ALL WORK AS SACRED VOCATION

In a general sense, all work, including the work of the political leader, has spiritual significance. An important contribution to our understanding of work came, when the priest, monk and reformer Martin Luther (1483 – 1546) liberated the notion of "calling" from the confines of cloistered walls where work was done by clerics and members of religious orders and extended it to include every type of work done by anyone and everyone. Luther wrote:

> ...the works of monks and priests, however holy and arduous they may be, do not differ one whit in the sight of God from the works of the rustic laborer in the field or the woman going about her household tasks...all works are measured before God by faith alone. [25]

Without regard to station in life, no matter how exciting or routine the work, no matter how important or mundane, whether done in public places in plain view of others or in private places that no one else sees, Luther reclaimed for all of us labor's true value as articulated by the 1st Century Christian Apostle Paul in his letter to the Corinthians: "whatever you do, do it all for the glory of God." [26]

This was a radical idea. Not only was all work given dignity, but each laborer was charged with the responsibility of doing his work for the glory of God. Now the sweat of his brow was a sacred offering at the altar of God. And this, of course, meant that political labor was also a sacred vocation.

---

[25] Martin Luther, *The Babylonian Captivity of the Church* (1520)

[26] 1 Corinthians 10:31

and that the work of the political leader was to be an offering at the altar of God.

Carried to its logical conclusion, doing one's work for the glory of God required one to do his work with the care, skill and precision that perhaps only God Himself would ever see or appreciate. It was not enough to satisfy the eye, the tastes, and the standards of other men and women, or of society. The implication of this for the political leader is enormous. For now, the political leader must do his or her work in such a way that God will be glorified by, and thus pleased with, the political leader's daily offering, even if the efforts which constitute the offering are never noticed or appreciated by anyone else. Now, what is done in secret has consequences, as if God is watching – which, in fact, He is.

POLITICS AS A SPECIAL CLASS OF SACRED VOCATION

Beyond the general sense of all work being a sacred vocation, politics is in a special class of vocation, with a unique, more demanding set of responsibilities. *"From everyone who has been given much, much will be demanded; and from the one who has been entrusted with much, much more will be asked."* [27]

No matter how high or low the office, the political leader stands in the shoes of the Sovereign God, personally invested with great power and with His Own Authority. The Sovereign God is the Good Shepherd of all seven billion plus men, women and children of earth; they are His Sheep. He does not just love Jews. He does not just love Christians. He loves every man, woman, boy and girl for they are His Creation and His Children. In the sense that every political leader is charged by the Good Shepherd with watching over and protecting His Sheep within that political leader's jurisdictional boundaries, the political leader is acting as a

---

[27] Luke 12:48

shepherd for the Sovereign God, and is fully accountable to Him for how he or she does his or her work.

Standing in the shoes of the Sovereign God for the purpose of watching over His Sheep, the political leader doesn't get to be whatever kind of political leader he or she wants to be. The political leader must measure up to the standards set by the Sovereign God, not by his or her own standards, or by the standards of his or her political crowd or party, or by the standards of the world – which frankly, are abysmally low, because our expectations of our political leaders have sunken to such woefully low levels.

That's the way the world of politics is meant to operate: as a sacred vocation in a holy arena. But it's a far cry from the current reality.

WHAT GOD HAS CALLED SACRED, POLITICAL LEADERS HAVE MADE PROFANE

Not all, but far too many political leaders around the world have made the sacred vocation of political leadership profane. By their personal conduct they have treated their sacred trust with abuse, irreverence and contempt. By how they go about their business, they have lowered the value and reputation of their calling, causing it to be viewed with contempt by those whom they are supposed to protect and serve.

The evidence for this sorry state of affairs is manifest. In almost every nation, polling indicates that a majority of people do not trust their political leaders to tell the truth, to do their jobs, or to deal with the most pressing issues facing the average man or woman, or their families.

It has never come as a surprise that authoritarian, top-down political systems such as have been the norm in communist countries for years are viewed by their people as nonresponsive and corrupt, existing to serve the interests of the economic and political elite. But in recent years even the United States, exemplar to the nations of what a liberal democracy should look like, has begun to bear all the marks of an oligarchy that exists to serve its economic and political elite. [28]

How in the world did the sacred vocation of political leader lose its sacredness?

It would be easy to blame the professionalization of politics, the rise of political consultants, the advent of the 24-hour news cycle, the coarsening of culture, the loss of civility. But those are mere contributing factors to a more fundamental cause.

The stripping of the sacred from the core of politics is the fruitless and counterproductive attempt by man to muscle the Sovereign God out of the Public Square, to substitute the internal and variable truths of man for the External and Eternal Truths of the Sovereign God, and to chart a course to the ever-elusive "progress" without a compass that points to the True North, which is the Sovereign God.

In the Twentieth Century, governments promoting state atheism, generally combined with active suppression of religious freedom and practice, officially denied the existence of God, as if they could legislate Him out of existence. And just to make sure He didn't meddle in their affairs, they persecuted, jailed, even murdered those who believed otherwise. While some of those nations have backed away from an official state atheism, they continue to be openly hostile to anyone and everyone who believes in the Sovereign God of the Bible. Belief in a Sovereign God is one of the most dangerous and subversive ideas known to authoritarian political leaders, for God or no God, the audacious idea that the governed might have allegiance to a higher authority than the state is a frightening prospect indeed.

Europe has devised a less sinister, but equally fruitless and counter-productive way of dealing with the Sovereign

---

[28] Martin Gilens and Benjamin I. Page, *"Testing Theories of American Politics: Elites, Interest Groups and Average Citizens,"* April 9, 2014, Princeton University

God. They officially ignore Him as if He doesn't exist, or if He does exist, as if He doesn't matter. They write Him out of their laws and constitutions. They banish reference to Him or to His External and Eternal Truths in the Public Square. They ridicule as anachronistic simpletons those who believe that the Sovereign God exists or has any business meddling in their business.

The United States has historically been a bastion of belief, welcoming the Sovereign God into the Public Square. But under a decades-long assault by militant atheism, it is no longer fashionable or politically correct to inject into the Public Square talk of the Sovereign God or of his External and Eternal Truths. So-called "enlightened" moderns believe that faith is a private matter which must be kept locked up at home or behind the closed doors of what they would refer to as that "quaint and irrelevant institution" – the church.

In some nations, the name of the Sovereign God or some weak imitation of Him has been commandeered by political leaders, and by terrorists masquerading as legitimate political leaders, for the purpose of oppressing and killing their opponents. But even though His Name might be invoked, it does not mean that He sanctions the oppression or killing. In fact, He abhors and condemns it. The political leaders who engage in such practices will have a special "reward" at the Day of Judgment, but it is not likely to be the "reward" they had hoped for.

As the sacred vocation of politics has become less sacred, either intentionally or through benign neglect, economic, social and political woes have multiplied and magnified. The woes are piling up like garbage that doesn't get picked up. The stench is stifling and will get worse.

This is all the natural result of political systems that cut their people and political leaders off from the blessings and protection of the Sovereign God, and from His External and Eternal Truths. The Sovereign God has not abandoned anyone. He has been abandoned by His People and by their political leaders.

The Sovereign God's Inexorable Plan for the Redemption of Man is on track and it will neither be changed nor stopped. The specifics of His Timetable may be a mystery to us, but it is most assuredly on schedule.

The Sovereign God asserts not only His right to be in the Public Square, He asserts His Ownership over it. He invites all men, women and children into His Square to dialogue, to peacefully work out their differences, and to solve their common problems. He asserts His Lordship over every aspect of the affairs of man, including politics, economics, government, and international relations.

The Sovereign God is about to put the political house in order throughout the world, deposing those political leaders who have made a mockery of their sacred vocation, who have neglected the welfare of the Sovereign God's Sheep, who have used their power and position to oppress them, and who have used their power and position to line their own pockets and the pockets of their friends, patrons and cronies.

The Day of Reckoning is at hand.
The Kingdom of God is coming.

Can you not see it?
Can you not hear it?

CHAPTER 4

THE SOVEREIGNTY OF GOD

*The Most High God is sovereign over all
kingdoms on earth and sets over them anyone
he wishes.* [29]

*For what else is the life of man but a kind of
play in which men in various costumes perform
until the director motions them offstage?* [30]

*The seventh angel sounded his trumpet, and
there were loud voices in heaven, which said:
"The kingdom of the world has become the
kingdom of our Lord and of his Messiah, and
he will reign for ever and ever."* [31]

"Sovereign God" is not an honorary title – a title given out of respect but without conferring any real powers, duties, or responsibilities. In fact, no one gave the Sovereign God that title at all. Rather it is a description of His Essential Nature.

HOW IS GOD SOVEREIGN?

At the most fundamental level, God is Sovereign because He can do anything He wants to do, whenever He

---

[29] Daniel 5:21

[30] Erasmus, *In Praise of Folly* (1511)

[31] Revelation 11:15

wants to do it, and however He chooses to do it. His Plans and Decisions are not subject to anyone's review or approval. They are not subject to anyone's veto. They are never put to a vote. Once He makes a decision, the matter is settled. There is no avenue of appeal.

He is not one god among many gods; He is the ONLY God there is. All other "gods" exist solely in the hearts and the imaginations of men and women.

As the Sovereign God, He is not merely "a higher power," He is THE Source of All Power. By His Law and by His Will He literally makes the world go round, keeps the planets in their orbits, and sustains life on earth. Without Him there would be chaos. Without Him there would be nothing at all. Without Him man would not even exist.

As the Sovereign God, He has absolute authority to rule over the affairs of men and women, for He IS the Source of All Authority. It is His absolute and exclusive right to delegate authority to earth's political leaders. And when it suits His Will, serves His Purposes and furthers His Plan, it is His absolute and exclusive right to take their authority away from any of them, or from all of them.

The Sovereign God is not merely one actor among many actors in the drama of history. He has been its Central Character from the moment the curtain went up at Creation, and He will be its Central Character until the moment when the final curtain comes down at the Day of Judgment. All men, women and children – and all political leaders at every level in every nation – are merely bit players who play their assigned parts and make their entrances and exits according to the stage directions given by Him, at such times as He directs.

While the Sovereign God gives men, women and children – and political leaders – the freedom to make good or bad choices, and to govern themselves, that freedom is always constrained by the boundaries that He has set, and which He enforces.

As the Great Law Giver, He establishes for their benefit the law within which every man, woman and child must live. And He establishes the consequences they must face, now or in the hereafter, if they choose to break the law. No one who breaks the law can choose to be exempt from the consequences. The only hope is that the Great Law Giver will show them mercy. And, as the Sovereign God, He is free to judge whomever He wishes to judge and He is free to show mercy to whomever He wishes to show mercy. He owes man nothing, yet every man, woman and child owes Him everything. Mercy is His gift to give, not man's right to claim.

While the law is designed so that men, women and children will be blessed if they obey it, the law reflects the essential character of the Sovereign God as a Just and Holy God. Because men and women in the Old Testament era began to burden themselves and each other with legalistic interpretations of the law, He boiled it down to two simple laws enunciated by Jesus as an expression of the essence of all the law and prophets: (1) *Love the Lord your God with all your heart and with all your soul and with all your mind* [32] and (2) *Love your neighbor as yourself.* [33] These are not suggestions. These are not recommendations. They ARE the law.

While the Sovereign God gives us much latitude to act in the political, economic and social spheres, He has written the basic story line of history and has already written its closing chapter. As much as men and women like to think they control their individual and corporate destiny, it is the Sovereign God who bends the arc of history according to His Will alone, to serve His Purposes alone, and to Further His Inexorable Plan for the Redemption of Man. The end of the story has never been in doubt. It will end just as He has said it

---

[32] Matthew 22:37

[33] Matthew 22:39

will end.

Simply put, the Sovereign God of the Bible has no rival. He has no equal. [34]

WITH ALL THAT UNCHECKED POWER, IS THE SOVEREIGN GOD A TYRANT?

Absolutely not!

In the hands of mortal, sinful men and women, such absolute, all-encompassing, unchecked power would, in fact, be dangerous. In the Hands of the Just and Holy God, man is absolutely safe.

Although He has absolute power and authority, He is not arbitrary. The Sovereign God does not act based on random choice or a personal whim. He unwaveringly and unfailingly acts to further His Inexorable Plan for the Redemption of Man.

Although there is no one capable of limiting or restraining His exercise of power and authority, the Sovereign God is not capricious. He is not given to sudden and unaccountable changes of mood or behavior. He is *"the same yesterday and today and forever."* [35] He does not change. [36] His *"word ... is eternal; it stands firm in the heavens."* [37]

Although He has the absolute right and authority to judge every man, woman and child – including every political leader – as harshly as He deems fit, and as harshly as they probably deserve, He *"is merciful and forgiving, even though [they] have rebelled against him."* [38]

---

[34] Isaiah 40:25

[35] Hebrews 13:8

[36] Malachi 3:6

[37] Psalm 119:89

[38] Daniel 9:9

Most importantly, such incredible power and authority can safely be entrusted to a Sovereign God who is not just loving, but who *"is love "*[39] As powerful as He is, as busy as He must be, yet He makes the time to know every man, woman, boy and girl. He knows their names. His knowledge of them is so intimate that He has numbered the hairs on each of their heads. [40] He knows their dreams, their aspirations, their longings, their fears. He hears and responds to them when they call upon His name. He is ready, willing and *"able to do immeasurably more than all we ask or imagine, according to his power that is at work within us. "*[41]

But the ultimate measure of what a Pure, Holy, Trustworthy, Merciful and Loving God He is was this: *"For God so loved the world that he gave his one and only Son, that whoever believes in him shall not perish but have eternal life. "* [42] He does not want anyone to perish [43] and actively searches for the lost. [44]

> *[In truth, dear reader, He loves YOU so much that if you were the only person on earth who needed to be rescued from sin and eternal death, He would still have surrendered Himself to the political authorities to be tried, convicted, beaten, humiliated, then crucified on the Cross.]*

Can a Sovereign God such as this be trusted with unlimited power and authority? Absolutely!

---

[39] 1 John 4:8

[40] Matthew 10:30

[41] Ephesians 3:20

[42] John 3:16

[43] 2 Peter 3:9

[44] Luke 15:1-7

HOW DOES HE EXERCISE HIS SOVEREIGNTY IN THE POLITICAL ARENA?

The Sovereign God puts political leaders in their positions of power and authority. And when it suits His Will, when it serves His Purposes, and when it furthers His Plan, He deposes them.

He raises up and commissions prophets to speak truth to power, to warn them to turn away from their evil acts, to confront them for their wickedness, and to announce divine judgment on them: for example, Moses, Elijah, Samuel, Isaiah, Jeremiah, Ezekiel, Daniel, Hosea, Jonah, and John the Baptist.

And once the warning is given and the judgment is announced, those political leaders who do not turn away from their evil acts, who do not repent of their wrongful conduct, will have their armies defeated, will lose all their power, will be stripped of their authority, will lose all their wealth, will lose their position, and may even lose their lives. When the political house is out of order, there is nothing the Sovereign God can't or won't do to restore justice, integrity, dignity, and virtue to the political order.

CHAPTER 5

GOVERNMENT FROM THE PERSPECTIVE OF THE SOVEREIGN GOD

If men were angels, no government would be necessary. [45]

Why has government been instituted at all? Because the passions of man will not conform to the dictates of reason and justice without constraint. [46]

Let everyone be subject to the governing authorities, for there is no authority except that which God has established. The authorities that exist have been established by God. [47]

FRAMING THE DEBATE

The debate over the proper role and size of government rages across the planet. It's not an issue unique to any particular political system.

In the best of times, in the most democratic of nations, the debate is carried out peacefully, yet with vigor and volume, in the corridors of political power, in the halls of justice, in the media, at organized public forums, at marches

---

[45] James Madison (1751 – 1836), 4th President of the United States (1809-1817)

[46] Alexander Hamilton (1755-1804), a Founding Father of the United States

[47] Romans 13:1

and rallies, and around family dinner tables.

In the worst of times, in every political system, the debate takes to the streets where the issues are contested, not with words, but with rocks, bottles, barricades, barbed wire, bullets, bayonets, tear gas, water cannons, incendiary devices, armored personnel carriers, tanks, and mass arrests.

In the most repressive and authoritarian of nations the public debate is silenced by threats of death, torture, forced labor camps, and lengthy, indefinite periods of imprisonment. Such states regularly silence the debate even in homes by demanding, as a test of loyalty to the state, that family members inform on one another for holding opinions that run counter to state-approved thought, for any deviation from state-mandated orthodoxy is, by definition, subversive. Even so, the debate cannot be silenced in the hearts and minds of man.

No matter where the debate takes place, no matter how peaceful or violent, no matter how free or repressive the political system, the debate is misinformed if it's not informed by a proper understanding of the origins, purpose, and limits of government as seen from the perspective of the Sovereign God.

TO ALL POLITICAL LEADERS OF EARTH: THIS IS THE WORD OF THE SOVEREIGN GOD TO YOU

THE PURPOSE OF CREATION

I am the Living God who created all that is, all that ever was, and all that will ever be. [48] *I am He of whom it is written that "the heavens declare the Glory of God; the skies proclaim the Work of His Hands."* [49]

---

[48] Genesis 1

[49] Psalm 19:1

I created man, male and female, in My Own Image. [50]
All men, women and children are the Jewels of My Creation.
They are the Objects of My Bounty. They are the Focus of My
Love. I did not bring the heavens and earth into existence for
their own sake, but as a home for man.

Not only am I a God of Love, I AM love. [51] *If you know*
love, then you know Me, even if you do not know My Name. If
you know not love, then you do not know Me at all. [52]

I created the sun, the moon, the stars, the air, the
waters, the farmlands, the mountains, the deserts, the fish of
the sea, the birds of the air, and every living creature that
moves on the ground as an offering of My Love for, and My
Blessing upon, man.

MAN AS SOCIAL AND POLITICAL CREATURE

I made men and women as social creatures who could
relate to Me and who could love Me as a genuine, heartfelt
and voluntary response to My Acts of Love extended towards
them. But inherent in the freedom to love Me was the
freedom to not love Me, even though men and women owed
Me for everything, including their very lives.

I made men and women as social creatures who would
also enjoy the friendship and companionship of one another,
their families, and neighbors. It is this social nature which
gave rise to the need of men and women to be political: to
find ways of relating to, and getting along with, each other; to
organize in order to promote the well-being of individuals,
families, and the social and political units in which they would
live; to regulate their own affairs and interactions; and to
provide for their common defense.

---

[50] Genesis 1:27

[51] 1 John 4:16

[52] 1 John 4:8

IN THE BEGINNING: DIRECT RULE BY GOD

I breathed life into the first man and woman and set them up in a garden which I created. It had everything they would ever need, or could ever want, so that they might enjoy an idyllic, safe and productive life.

In the beginning the first man and woman, Adam and Eve, lived under my direct, loving rule. So that they might enjoy the fruits of all that I had provided, I gave them two simple, straightforward laws by which they must live, one positive and one negative:

> *First, be fruitful and increase in number; fill the earth and subdue it; rule over the fish in the sea and the birds in the sky and over every living creature that moves on the ground.* [53]

> *Second you are free to eat from any tree in the garden; but you must not eat from the tree of the knowledge of good and evil, for when you eat from it you will certainly die.* [54]

A TEMPTING, BUT DEADLY IDEA: TO BE LIKE GOD

But Satan, in the guise of a snake, put into Eve's heart that I had an ulterior motive for keeping her and Adam from partaking of the tree of the knowledge of good and evil. He told her that if she and Adam would eat of the tree they would "be like God, knowing good and evil." [55]

To "be like God:" the desire of men and women that is at the root of all sin, the temptation that is at the root of all evil. The desire to substitute their own judgment for Mine. The desire to decide for themselves what is "true" without reference to My External Truth. The desire to make and live

---

[53] Genesis 1:28

[54] Genesis 1:16-17

[55] Genesis 3:5

by their own rules rather than by the rules of the LORD who is their Judge, their Lawgiver and King. [56] The desire to govern themselves without having to be accountable to anybody, even though there is One who demands accountability of everybody.

Finding the idea of self-sovereignty more appealing than God-centered sovereignty, first Eve, then Adam, ate of the forbidden fruit. In doing so, they rebelled against My Direct, Loving Rule.

Thus was the Fall of Man, by which sin was introduced into the world, and by which the walls were breached that protected man from evil. Even though they had enough of everything they could need or want, it wasn't enough for them. They were willing to break what they perceived to be "one little rule" to find out what I was holding back from them. To their dismay, they and their descendants would quickly discover what it was that I was holding back: it was death, destruction, chaos and evil. Though I had restrained these forces as an act of loving protection, by their rebellious act the first man and woman unleashed these forces upon themselves and upon the world.

SIN RIPPED THE FABRIC OF THE CREATED ORDER

The cost of the Fall for Adam and Eve was expulsion from the garden, lest they also eat of the tree of life and live forever. [57] And their descendants, which is every man, woman and child since that time, have been paying the price for their ancestors' willful disobedience.

The descendants are not being punished for the original sin of their ancestors; but they are exposed to the consequences of their ancestors' rebellious acts in the garden. For the fabric of the intended order, by which men and

---

[56] Isaiah 33:22

[57] Genesis 3:23

women were to live in fellowship, peace and harmony with Me and with each other, had been ripped apart.

After their banishment from the garden, the first murder took place when Cain, a son of Adam and Eve, usurped My Authority over life and death and killed his brother, Abel, because Cain was jealous and envious of him. [58]

The human race increased and spread. Nine generations later it had become completely wicked and obsessed with evil. Every inclination of the thoughts of the human heart was only evil all the time. [59] Man had become corrupt and had in turn corrupted the entire created order, filling the earth with violence. [60]

When I could no longer recognize My Own Image when I looked into the face of man, I determined to wipe the human race from the face of the earth – and with them the animals, the birds and the creatures that move along the ground, for I regretted that I had made them. [61]

But in the midst of my anger I took note of Noah, a righteous man, blameless among the people of his time who walked faithfully with Me. [62] I did not change My Mind about destroying man, for I am unchangeable, [63] but I was moved by love and compassion towards Noah and his family and resolved to show them mercy.

I saved them by directing Noah to build an ark, teaching him how to build it, then filling it up with a robust contingent of birds, animals and plants that would benefit Noah, his family, and future generations of mankind. The rest of My Creation, including the rest of mankind, I

---

[58] Genesis 4:2-8

[59] Genesis 6:5

[60] Genesis 6:11-12

[61] Genesis 6:7

[62] Genesis 6:9

[63] Malachi 3:6; James 1:17

destroyed by covering them with a great flood.

With this new beginning, I never gave a second thought to giving up on, and destroying, man who I had created in My Own Image. With this new start, I began to reveal the broad outline of My Inexorable Plan for the Redemption of Man, which is well underway and which will soon be fully realized.

HOW SHALL MAN BE CONSTRAINED?

Man rejected My Direct Rule. Man's sin disrupted and destabilized the order which I created. Man's rebellion introduced death, destruction and evil into the world. These conditions will persist until the Day of Reckoning, also called the Day of Judgment, a day which I have already fixed in time, and which will be here soon.

But the human race would not make it all the way to the predetermined Day of Reckoning if chaos went unchecked. Some semblance of order needed to be restored Figurative and literal boundaries, fences, and rules had to be established, and enforcement mechanisms instituted, if man was to survive what he had unleashed upon himself and the world by his own rebellion.

I was, I am, and I always will be, the only legitimate source of authority over the affairs of man. Yet from Adam and Eve forward, men and women have resisted living under My Direct Rule and Authority. Therefore, I have delegated to earthly rulers My Exclusive Right and Authority to govern the affairs of man.

Man does not govern the way I would. Yet I give as much latitude as possible to allow his earthly rulers and governments to work out how to organize themselves and to respond to the specific challenges that face them.

Yet I still influence the hearts and minds of man, and thus his affairs. And when I deem it necessary to serve My Purposes and to further My Plan, I raise up some political leaders and depose others. And I do it in My Own Time and according to My Own Will, not according to the desires or timetables of man.

THE NATURE AND LIMITS OF POLITICAL AUTHORITY

I am now, I was yesterday, and I will be forever the Sovereign God of the Universe. I have not abdicated My Throne and no one can depose Me.

Whatever authority you have to rule over the affairs of man is derivative: it comes exclusively from Me. It is not derived from the people, from their political leaders, from the elite, from brute force, from armies, or from political parties.

Whatever authority you have to rule over the affairs of man is delegated by Me to be used in accordance with My Will and Purposes; it is not given to you to do with as you please. Whatever authority you have to rule over the affairs of man is a matter of your stewardship, not your ownership.

I retain the absolute right to hold you personally accountable – in the here-and-now and in the hereafter – for the manner in which you exercise My Authority. And I retain the absolute right to revoke your authority with or without cause, with or without further notice, and without your consent or the consent of the governed, the elite, your armies, or anyone else.

While I give you some latitude to reason for yourself how best to exercise your delegated authority, you must exercise it in a way that honors Me and upholds the dignity of the governed, who have the status of Man Created In The Image Of God. And above all, you must not stand between Me and man, and you shall not attempt to substitute yourself or the state for Me.

THE DARK SIDE OF GOVERNMENT

I have sanctioned the institution of government so that good order can be maintained, so that chaos can be restrained, so that My Sheep can be safe, and so that political leaders (as their shepherds) can watch over them and provide for their well-being.

However, when ordinary men and women, prone to sin as they are, assume exalted positions as political leaders, they do not lay aside their sinful natures and become gentle as lambs. Rather, they are tempted to become as ravenous as wolves seeking more power and more control over the sheep. They are tempted to oppress "for the good of the sheep". They are tempted to overreach and encroach on areas that do not belong to them. They are tempted to believe that "they know what is best" for the sheep and that the sheep are ignorant of what is best for them.

Under My Direct Rule in the garden men and women were subject to only two laws. Under the rule of man, My Sheep are subjected to tens and hundreds of thousands of laws, rules and regulations.

HOW SHALL GOVERNMENT BE CONSTRAINED?

The greatest constraint on government is the very DNA of freedom that I gave man in the beginning. For as much as man rebelled against Me and My two simple laws in the garden, even more will man bridle under the restraint of tens and hundreds of thousands of laws, rules and regulations imposed by his fellow man.

Nonetheless, because all authorities that exist have been established by me I have commanded my people to subject themselves the governing authorities. [64] *I have further instructed them pray for their leaders, be they kings or others*

---

[64] Romans 13:1

in authority. [65]

RENDER UNTO CAESAR?

Earthly rulers are prone to overreach, sometimes with the best of intentions (believing they are doing what is right) and sometimes with the worst of intentions (because they are wicked oppressors). What is man to do?

You have heard it said "to give back to Caesar what is Caesar's, and to God what is God's." [66] *But the meaning has been misconstrued by some as justifying allowing Caesar, which signifies the ruling authorities, to do whatever Caesar pleases and the people must docilely accept it.*

First, I warn you earthly rulers to know your place, to know the limits of your authority. Tread lightly when ruling over My People. Do not overreach and encroach on domains that do not belong to you. Above all, do not oppress My People – perhaps the gravest of sins you can commit against Me.

Second, I say to My People: when earthly rulers overreach and encroach on domains reserved to Me, and which I have not given them over you, you are to resist them. Do so peacefully and prayerfully, but with irresistible determination. I will be with you in your struggle.

THE KINGDOM IS COMING

The Kingdom of God is coming. It is on its way and will be here sooner than you imagine. And when it arrives, it will sweep away ALL earthly kingdoms, all self-styled empires; while the Kingdom of God will endure forever.

---

[65] 1 Timothy 2:2

[66] Matthew 22:21

And the tens and hundreds of thousands of laws, rules and regulations of man's kingdoms will be swept away. And just as only two laws were needed in the garden, only two laws will be needed in the Kingdom of Heaven:

> *Love the Lord your God with all your heart and with all your soul and with all your mind;* [67] *and*
> *Love your neighbor as yourself.* [68]

As I have said it, so shall it be.

Amen

---

[67] Matthew 22:37

[68] Matthew 22:39

CHAPTER 6
THE SOVEREIGN GOD'S INVITATION TO ALL POLITICAL LEADERS

[H]ave the same mindset as Christ Jesus:

Who, being in very nature God, did not consider equality with God something to be used to his own advantage; rather, he made himself nothing by taking the very nature of a servant, being made in human likeness. [69]

TO ALL POLITICAL LEADERS OF EARTH: THIS IS THE WORD OF THE SOVEREIGN GOD TO YOU

I am the Almighty God of the Bible. I am not a mere character confined to the pages of a book. I am not a figment of the imagination of seers, prophets, and storytellers.

I am the Almighty God of History. I have written the storyline of history and I bend it according to My Will, to serve My Purposes, and to further My Inexorable Plan for the Redemption of Man.

Not only do I preside over the Kingdom of God, which will be here soon to sweep away and replace all earthly kingdoms, My Lordship extends to all kingdoms of earth including the political jurisdiction where you exercise authority.

---

[69] Philippians 2:5-7

I am the Source of All Authority. Any and all authority which you have is derived from, and delegated by, Me. I have entrusted it to your care as a matter of stewardship; it is not yours to possess, to own, or to use for whatever purposes you choose. You are accountable to Me for how you use My Authority.

Worldwide the political house of man is in disarray. I am coming very soon to put things in order. Those political leaders who resist or oppose Me will be swept away into the dust bin of history. Those who bow down before Me and serve Me will be exalted.

I do not seek your support as an ally, for that would accord you the status of My Equal, of which I have none save Christ Jesus, the Son of the Living God. Rather I extend My Invitation for you to become My Servant.

All people of earth, including all who dwell in your political jurisdiction, are created in My Own Image. They are the Jewels of My Creation, the Objects of My Bounty, and the Focus of My Love. Not only would I do anything for them, but I have already sacrificed My Son on the Cross so that the grip of sin and death on humankind would be broken.

I am the Shepherd for all of My People. As a political leader of earth, I call you to be a shepherd for those of My People over whom you exercise My Authority.

As a shepherd you will be charged with the responsibility of leading My Sheep to green pastures where they may get the nourishment they need and to quiet waters where they may refresh their souls. And when wolves threaten the flock, you shall beat the wolves with your rod and staff, and scatter them into the forest.

As My Shepherd you will not be tasked with watching over only Some of My Sheep within your jurisdictional boundaries, but over All of My Sheep therein. You are to be impartial in your care for the entire flock. Your justice and benevolence is to be extended to all in equal measure.

As My Servant, and as the Shepherd of My Flock, when you look into the faces of the men, women and children entrusted to your care, you shall see My Image reflected in every one of them, regardless of who they are, regardless of their social or economic status, regardless of where they come from, regardless of the color of their skin, regardless of the language they speak, regardless of whether or not they can do anything for you. For each is of equal value in My Sight, and you shall treat them accordingly.

As a political leader who serves Me and serves My People, do not shrink from war, but also do not be eager to run towards it. Study peace and constantly pursue it. Learn and apply the skills of diplomacy. Acquire and practice the skills of problem-solving, conflict resolution and compromise.

Treat your work as a sacred vocation. Give glory to Me in how you do your work, whether in public or in secret, and you will be a blessing to My People.

Do not limit your skill set to those skills required to secure and maintain your position as a political leader. Rather, learn how to be a truly effective political leader. Learn how to the get the things done that My People need to have done by their political leaders.

Commit yourself to being a self-aware leader so that you will know your own shortcomings and to identify what more you need in order to compensate for, or overcome, your shortcomings. Do not settle for "good enough" to get into office, or to stay in office. Strive for excellence in office.

Commit yourself to becoming a virtuous political leader. Make a life-long commitment to learning what it means to be a virtuous political leader. Make a life-long commitment to developing and practicing the habits that develop virtue.

Learn and practice the virtue of humility. Study the example of Christ Jesus who, though He was in the very nature God, did not take advantage of His Status, but took upon Himself the role of a Servant. [70] *Many political leaders learn how to ACT humble, at least in public. But I call you to learn how to actually BE humble at all times, whether in the Public Square or in private places.*

Commit yourself to a life of integrity, in which there is no gap between your actions and what you say you stand for. There is a dearth of integrity in the practice of politics worldwide, and it has led the people to lose faith and trust in their political leaders, in the political process, and in the very institutions which hold societies together.

Learn to be a magnanimous leader who lifts the vision of the people to accomplish great things together, and summons the better angels of their nature.

Do what you know to be right, [71] *even if it is not popular. Do not do what you know to be wrong, just because it will please others or shield you from their criticism.*

Have courage and backbone to the point that you are willing to sacrifice your political career for the sake of doing what you know to be right.

Learn and practice self-control, [72] *lest you become controlled by your own ambition and passions, leading to your inevitable ruin, shame and humiliation.*

Be passionate about the cause of justice, for I am a Just God. I hate injustice [73] *and demand that earthly rulers both act justly and actively pursue justice.* [74]

Neither participate in corruption, nor turn a blind eye to it, for I am not corrupt. I detest corruption [75] *and demand that earthly rulers detest it too, and that they actively seek to root it out.*

---

[70] Philippians 2:5-7

[71] Proverbs 21:3; Genesis 4:7

[72] Titus 2:11-12

[73] Proverbs 6:16-19

[74] Psalm 82:2

[75] Proverbs 8:13

Surround yourself with advisors, [76] *strategists, staff, and key volunteers who are both effective and virtuous, for lesser men and women will bring you down to their level.* [77]

Do not be puffed up with your own sense of self-importance. [78] *What you do is important, but who you are is not. Practice your political profession as a sacred vocation, not as a victory lap in celebration of yourself.*

Resist the temptations and trappings inherent in your profession. Do not do what everybody else does, or what you think everybody else does, just because they seem to get away with it. Be free of any sense of entitlement. Do what you know to be right. [79] *Do not do what you know to be wrong, even though the likelihood of getting caught is low and the consequences are minimal. Do not do what you know to be wrong, regardless of whether anyone is watching ... for I am always watching and I read your heart and your mind. You have no secrets from Me.*

Commit yourself to acting in such a way that you, and your office, will merit the respect and trust of My People. If you earn their respect and trust, you will likely please Me.

I know every challenge you face. I know that you are in a profession that is ego-bruising, often brutish, all-consuming, sometimes dehumanizing, and always rough-and-tumble. I do not minimize the difficulties you deal with every day.

But the political arena today is not much different than the political arena in which My Beloved Servant King David operated. He rose. He stumbled. He fell. And I forgave him and helped him regain his footing. He was far from perfect, but he had a perfect love for Me. His moral armor had chinks in it, but he strove to be a virtuous leader of My People.

---

[76] Proverbs 15:22

[77] 1 Corinthians 15:33

[78] Isaiah 14:12-15; 1 Peter 5:8

[79] Genesis 4:7

I call you to strive to be perfect [80] and a virtuous leader, but I know you will stumble and fall. If you have a perfect love for Me, I will forgive you and I will help you regain your footing. But I do call you to do your very best, not just "good enough" to get by.

If you lack wisdom, you should ask Me. I give generously to all without finding fault; the wisdom which you seek will be given to you. [81]

I want you to succeed because I love you and because I want you to be a blessing to My People.

Accept my invitation to serve Me and to be a Servant-Shepherd of My People. If you will sincerely approach your calling as an effective and virtuous political leader, I will bless you both in the here-and-now and in the hereafter.

As I have said it, so shall it be.

Amen

---

[80] Matthew 5:48

[81] James 1:5

CHAPTER 7

THE SOVEREIGN GOD'S WARNING TO ALL POLITICAL LEADERS

*[T]his is what the Lord, the God of Israel, says
to the shepherds who tend my people: "Because
you have scattered my flock and driven them
away and have not bestowed care on them, I will
bestow punishment on you for the evil you have
done," declares the Lord. "I myself will gather
the remnant of my flock out of all the countries
where I have driven them and will bring them
back to their pasture, where they will be fruitful
and increase in number. I will place shepherds
over them who will tend them, and they will no
longer be afraid or terrified, nor will any be
missing," declares the Lord.* [82]

TO ALL POLITICAL LEADERS OF EARTH:
THIS IS THE WORD OF THE SOVEREIGN GOD TO YOU

*The words which I spoke through My Servant Jeremiah
were specific to the political leaders of My People Israel more
than two millennia ago. But now I give a similar warning to
you.*

*While My Covenant Relationship with Israel is
unbroken, My Lordship extends to all humankind, for all*

---

[82] Jeremiah 23: 2-4

men, women and children, are created in My Own Image, as the Jewels of My Creation, as the Objects of My Bounty, and as the Focus of My Love.

I am sovereign over all the kingdoms of earth. [83] No kingdom is too small or too big, none too poor or too rich, none too weak or too powerful, none too remote or too insignificant, to escape my attention or concern.

I am the Source of All Power and Authority. No nation, no earthly ruler, no army, no economy, no alliance or axis of powers, is too big or too strong for Me to bring down, for I am the Sovereign God. [84]

I am about to set the political house in order throughout the world, and I am fully able to do so.

If you reject My Invitation to bow down before Me and to serve Me, to be or to become an effective and virtuous shepherd worthy of watching over, serving and protecting the Children of the Sovereign God, then I will remove you and replace you with someone who will be such a shepherd.

I am fully willing and able to bring to their knees, to depose and to crush kings and queens, princes and princesses, presidents, prime ministers, party chairmen, "dear leaders", "supreme leaders", fuehrers, generals, and any other real or self-imagined leader, no matter how glorified their title. [85] To Me you are no more troublesome than a fly buzzing about the tail of a cow.

If you are a virtuous political leader but completely lacking in the skills, intellectual discipline, and self-regulation essential to doing the work to which I have called you, then get those skills, acquire that intellectual discipline, and start regulating yourself. But do it quickly for you do not have much time. And if you are either unwilling or unable to do so, then leave the political arena now or I will allow the

---

[83] Psalm 47:7-9

[84] Isaiah 40:23-25

[85] Daniel 2:21

political jackals to have their way with you, to devour your political carcass. While your soul may be precious to Me, you being the one to occupy a specific position of political leadership is not essential to My Plan.

No matter how "effective" you may be at "getting things done", if you are utterly lacking in the basic virtues required of one who wears the mantle of the Sovereign God's Authority, then get out of the way before I move you out of the way and replace you with someone who is both effective and virtuous.

If you consistently make a fool of yourself and a mockery of your office by engaging in shameful and disreputable conduct unworthy of one who is clothed with the Mantle of My Authority, then cease such conduct before I throw you out in a display of Divine Disgust that will eclipse anything the press could do to embarrass you.

If you cannot, or will not, harness your ambition for good, then you are of no use to Me, to My People, or to My Kingdom. Get out of the political arena while there is yet time.

If you enjoy engaging in political theater more than in getting anything of significance done, then exit the political stage now, before I sweep you into the dust bin of history, for I am neither entertained nor impressed by your theatrics.

If you are so ineffective and so self-serving that the people whom you govern have lost faith in you, then you have exhausted My Patience. If you are unable or unwilling to become an effective servant-leader of My People, or are unable or unwilling to do it in short order, then it would be best for you to leave office now before My Heavenly Sergeant-At-Arms shows you the door and unceremoniously tosses you into the street.

I am keeping track of all political leaders. I am taking note of those who have been derelict in their duties, absorbed with advancing or protecting their own careers, obsessed by the pursuit of position and power for the sake of nothing more than their own self-preservation, self-advancement and self-glorification. Soon your worries will be over, for you will have no political career to protect, for I will end it abruptly and with no more notice than has been given here.

If you have turned a blind eye to injustice and corruption, or, worse yet, have engaged in, and encourage, injustice and corruption, woe be unto you. Repent now and change your course of conduct immediately before I expose you and turn you over to the political jackals, or worse yet, before I let the people whom you were supposed to be serving have their way with you.

If you love the game of politics more than you love Me, or the governed whom I have entrusted to your care, then it would have been better that you had never entered the political arena, for your exit will be neither sweet nor pleasant.

If you love your own reflected glory more than you love the reflection of the Living God seen in the faces of the men, women and children whom I have created and whom you are called to serve, then withdraw from the political arena now before I show you and the world how repellant to Me your reflection has become.

If you are more interested in using the powers and tools of governing to benefit yourself and your wealthy and powerful friends, donors, and cronies, than in using those powers and tools to promote the welfare of the governed, especially the weak and the powerless, then prepare to lose everything for I will strip you, your friends, your donors, and you cronies of everything you possess, including your last shred of dignity.

If you are an authoritarian, oppressor, tyrant or thug who seeks to force a yoke upon the necks of the men, women and children whom I have created, who I love, then you stand in direct opposition to Me. I have reserved a special place for you near the Center of the Flames of Hell where I have dispatched a multitude of other authoritarians, oppressors, tyrants and thugs who have preceded you. Repent now and you will merely lose your position and power, but not your soul. Do not repent and you will lose your life, your position, your power, and your soul.

* * * * * * * * * *

TO MY PEOPLE: Pray for the success of political leaders in your community, your nation, and around the world who are both effective AND virtuous – whether you know who they are, or not. Pray for the deposing of all political leaders who are neither effective nor virtuous, no matter where they may be, for they are a cancer and a scourge which must be eradicated.

The battle lines between those who side with the Armies of the Sovereign God and those who side with the powers and principalities of darkness and evil are forming. The trumpet call to battle is now sounded. The outcome is not in doubt. But the battle will be terrible.

I am coming to your rescue. Stand firm and watch prayerfully and expectantly for what I am about to do. Neither be afraid nor discouraged, for I will be there soon and I will make all things right.

* * * * * * * * * *

TO ALL OF HUMANITY: Behold the Day of Reckoning, the Day of Judgment, is upon you. The Kingdom of God is at hand.

As I have said it, so shall it be.

Amen.

CHAPTER 8

IF A POLITICAL LEADER DOESN'T BELIEVE THE MESSAGE

"Then they will know that I am the Lord." [86]

The Spirit of the Lord directs me to speak in my own voice to those political leaders who don't believe in the Sovereign God. While I don't put aside my prophetic role or responsibility, and I always speak from the perspective of faith, let me speak to you now as one political insider to another.

You and I make political calculations every day:
- What's the upside? What's the downside?
- What are the rewards? What are the risks?
- Who's ox will get gored? Will my ox get gored?
- Who's on what side of the issue?
- What's the political cost to saying yes? What's the political cost of saying no?
- Is there a way I can have my cake and eat it too?

Such political calculations are one of the things that ordinary citizens understand the least, yet hate the most about the business of politics, but it's the nature of the beast.

The entire Bible, from first page to last, declares the Lordship of the Sovereign God over history from start to finish, and over the affairs of all men and all nations.

Over the course of 1,273 verses in 48 chapters, the prophet Ezekiel emphatically declares 65 times in one form

---

[86] Ezekiel 7:27

or another the resolve of the Sovereign God to be known and to be acknowledged: *"Then they will know that I am the Lord."* [87]

In the Old Testament the Sovereign God says: *"By myself I have sworn, my mouth has uttered in all integrity a word that will not be revoked: Before me every knee will bow; by me every tongue will swear."* [88] Those words are echoed in the New Testament where the Apostle Paul reports what God had said centuries earlier: *"Surely as I live,"* says the Lord, *"every knee shall bow before me, every tongue will acknowledge God."* [89]

The Sovereign God already knows you, but He wants you to know Him. He wants you to bow down before and acknowledge Him as God. He wants you to serve Him.

Soon enough YOU WILL hear His Voice, YOU WILL see His Mighty Acts, and YOU WILL meet Him face to face. But by that time, I regret to inform you, it will probably be too late for you to change course and escape the Day of Reckoning, also known as the Day of Judgment, with either your life or your soul.

I'm not trying to be threatening here. Rather I'm trying to persuade you to take another look at the Sovereign God ... while there is still time.

THE REASON(S) WHY YOU MAY NOT BELIEVE

There are political leaders who don't believe that there's a God at all. This may be a matter of thoughtful deliberation or it may be a reflection of their upbringing and/or the spirit of the culture in which they were raised and now live.

---

[87] Ezekiel 7:27

[88] Isaiah 45:23

[89] Romans 14:11

There are political leaders who are willing to believe that all that they see around them, and all that's ever been, is the product of one great cosmic accident and that there's nothing and no one "out there" who could care one whit about what humans, their political leaders, or their governments do.

There are political leaders who are willing to admit to the possibility that someone or something created the world, but that whoever or whatever he, she or it was, has moved on to other creative projects in the cosmos and is no longer concerned with what goes on here on earth.

There are political leaders who believe in some abstract concept of God, but they believe that "God" or "god" is more of a comforting idea that exists in our hearts and heads than a real person or personage who has much of anything to do with, or say about, how we humans manage our daily affairs as individuals, families, or as nations.

There are political leaders who are acquainted with the stories and general claims of the Bible, but they believe them to be legends, products of primitive imaginations, devices of moralists and storytellers seeking to explain that which can be explained in no other way. Or the more sinister explanation: devices used by the powerful to keep the masses sedated and compliant.

There are more variations of nonbelief but it's not useful to catalog them all here.

WHAT YOU CHOOSE TO BELIEVE DOESN'T ALTER REALITY

God is God, whether you choose to believe in Him or not.

The Sovereign God is Lord and Master of the Universe, and also of your smaller, less-universal, less-significant political jurisdiction, whether you like it or not.

He is King of Kings and Lord of Lords; you're His Subordinate, whether you admit to it or not.

You can try to ignore Him, but He isn't going away.

You can try to deny Him voice in the Public Square, but He will not, and cannot, be silenced.

You can puff up your chest, beat on it, shake your fist and weaponry, and offer up a blood-curdling war whoop, trying to impress or scare Him. If you're lucky He will merely laugh. If you're not lucky, ... well, just use your imagination.

You can boast all you want about the power and might that you and your army, navy, and air force possess, but it doesn't change the fact that He can merely blow on you and you will wither, after which a whirlwind will sweep you away like chaff. [90]

You can try to build walls and fences to keep Him out but He has never been hindered by man-made walls or fences; not even by massive oceans, formidable mountain ranges, mighty rivers, or the deepest and widest canyons.

His upper-case Kingdom of God is coming soon and it will sweep away your lower-case kingdom of man, whether you believe it or not.

The Day of Reckoning, the Day of Judgment, is just around the corner and you have no power to stop the clock or move the date.

I'm hoping that by now you're asking yourself, "What if what he says in this book is actually true?"

AN OFFER (I HOPE) YOU CAN'T REFUSE

If you bet that I'm wrong, and it turns out that everything that's been said in this book is true, then you haven't simply bet on "the wrong side of history," you've bet against the Sovereign God of the Universe Who created you, who allowed you to exercise His Authority as a political leader, and Who is about to judge you and determine your fate for all eternity.

---

[90] Isaiah 40:24

It's my preference, and it is the desire of the Sovereign God, that you simply bow your knee before Him now as an act of submission, and that you acknowledge Him this very instant as the Sovereign God, Your King, and Your Lord.

However, if you still have doubts about the message that's been delivered, the invitation that's been extended, or the warning that's been issued, you may not be ready to do that … yet.

Speaking as I would if I were one of your most trusted advisors, I urge you to consider hedging your bet, minimizing your risk. As a political leader at any level, in any nation, I know you do this dozens of times a day. It's your political instinct to do so.

You need to ask yourself:

- What's the downside (if any) of my living as if everything that's been written in this book is true?
- What's the upside of my accepting "God's Invitation to ALL Political Leaders" as set forth in Chapter 6?
- Can there possibly be <u>any</u> downside to my committing to being a more effective political leader?
- What's the reward for my committing to being a virtuous political leader?
- What's the risk (if any) of becoming a true servant leader of the people whom I govern?
- Who could seriously criticize me for developing a passion for justice?
- Could anyone possibly say that being an enemy of corruption is a bad thing?

If you're still leaning against believing the message, accepting the invitation, and heeding the warning, let me get more earthy and remind you of an iconic scene in the 1971 movie *Dirty Harry.* [91] As San Francisco detective Harry Callahan (played by Clint Eastwood) stands over a wounded bank robber laying on the ground within inches of his gun, Harry puts the bank robber's next decision in perspective:

> *I know what you're thinking, punk. You're thinking "did he fire six shots or only five?" Now to tell you the truth I forgot myself in all this excitement. But being this is a .44 Magnum, the most powerful handgun in the world and will blow your head clean off, you've gotta ask yourself a question: "Do I feel lucky?" Well, do ya, punk?*

My question to you, dear political leader, is this: "Do you feel lucky?"

While the political jackals may begin to circle because they mistake virtue for weakness, the people whom you govern will love you and will rally to your side if you are both virtuous and effective. More importantly, the Sovereign God will look upon you with favor and He will help you to fight off, and defeat, all jackals, wolves, and other political predators. You couldn't have a more powerful or valuable ally.

If today you could speak with Cyrus the Great, King of Persia (559–530 BC), he would tell you (with the benefit of 2600 years of hindsight) that he owed his success as one of history's greatest military leaders and empire builders to the Sovereign God who chose to use Cyrus to carry out God's larger purposes in history. [92] And the Sovereign God chose him as his "anointed servant" and used him even "though you [Cyrus] do not acknowledge me." [93]

---

[91] *Dirty Harry* (1971), Copyright © MCMLXXI by Warner Bros. Inc. and The Malpaso Company

[92] Isaiah 44:24 – 48:22

[93] Isaiah 45:4

If you accept the proposition offered here, the Sovereign God will bless you and use you as a political leader to accomplish His larger purposes in history. And while doing so, you'll get to know Him and you'll learn from first-hand experience that all that's been said here about Him and His Kingdom is true. As you experience His Help and His Love, I'm willing to bet that you begin to "love the LORD your God with all your heart and with all your soul and with all your strength." [94]

And the deeper, the more perfect, your love for Him, He will bless you both as an individual and as a political leader:

> *"For the eyes of the LORD run to and fro throughout the whole earth, to show himself strong on behalf of those whose heart is perfect towards him."* [95]

IF YOU REFUSE THIS OFFER

However, if you think this is all nonsense and you refuse the offer, my final plea is that you re-read Chapter 7: "God's Warning to ALL Political Leaders."

Meanwhile your staff, your strategists, your friends, your supporters, even you cronies, may want to head for the exits before the Sovereign God starts to "deal" with you, and they become collateral damage.

---

[94] Deuteronomy 6:5

[95] 2 Chronicles 16:9

CHAPTER 9

A FINAL MESSAGE TO POLITICAL LEADERS: "A TIME TO CHOOSE"

But if serving the Lord seems undesirable to you, then choose for yourselves this day whom you will serve.... But as for me and my household, we will serve the Lord." [96]

As directed by the Sovereign God, I have performed (and will continue to perform) the three tasks initially given to me: (1) to deliver His message to ALL political leaders of earth; (2) to extend His invitation to them; and (3) to issue His warning to those who reject the invitation.

Now the Hand of the Lord is upon me and He has expanded my mandate to include a fourth task with three parts, two of which will be fulfilled in this chapter and the third in the next.

THE "ENDGAME" OF HISTORY HAS BEGUN

The first part of the fourth task is simultaneously joyful and dreadful: *to announce that the "endgame" of history has begun.*

The curtain is already rising on the Final Act of the Human Drama, at the conclusion of which history as we understand it will end, and eternity (which we cannot yet comprehend) will begin. As dramatic was the Creation, the ending will be equally dramatic with:

---

[96] Joshua 24:15

- The Day of Reckoning, or Day of Judgment, which no man or woman, living or dead, can escape – a glorious day for those who have aligned themselves with the Sovereign God, and a horrifying day for those who have aligned themselves against the Sovereign God.
- The Second Coming of the Risen Christ, the Son of the Living God, who at the meridian of history broke the power of death by offering himself as a substitutionary sacrifice on behalf of each and every man, woman and child, both the living and the dead.
- The arrival of the Kingdom of God which shall endure for all of eternity under the righteous reign of the Son of God, a kingdom which will require only two laws: (1) *Love the Lord your God with all your heart and with all your soul and with all your mind* [97] and (2) *Love your neighbor as yourself.* [98]

It is a joyful task because those who are disciples of Jesus Christ have been watching and waiting for this day for more than two thousand years. Every generation of the faithful has lived as if this day might come at any moment. Their steadfast faith, despite hardships, suffering, and persecution, will soon be vindicated.

It is a dreadful task for two reasons. First, much of what will take place during the Final Act, and before its dramatic conclusion, will be dreadful and will affect every nation. Even those protected by the Sovereign God will be shocked and horrified to witness what unfolds. It has not been revealed to me, nor will it be, the timing, the details of what will happen, or the sequence of events – such details are extraneous to my prophetic mandate. Besides, such matters are amply

---

[97] Matthew 22:37

[98] Matthew 22:39

described in the apocalyptic visions of Daniel [99] and John of Patmos. [100] Even if they were revealed to me, it's doubtful that my powers of observation or description could bring much clarity to events that are so far beyond the limits of my comprehension and imagination. But from this moment forward, I will daily *"keep watch, because [I] do not know on what day [the] Lord will come."* [101]

The second reason the task is dreadful is that millions and millions of people will lose their lives, and likely their souls, if they are aligned against the Sovereign God, or if they delude themselves into thinking that they can remain neutral and not take a stand for God or against Him.

A LINE IN THE SAND

The second part of the fourth task is to draw a line in the sand. I am to then invite all political leaders of earth, of every nation, of every level, to choose a side of the line on which to stand.

On one side of the line I will invite to stand those political leaders who choose to bow down, worship, and serve the Living God, who is Sovereign over the entire Universe, over all nations, over every aspect of the affairs of man, and over every man, woman and child. They may be imperfect political leaders, but these are the ones willing to commit themselves to being as godly, as effective and as virtuous as they can possibly be – with the exceedingly generous love and help of the One Who Calls Them to Serve. He will be their wisdom. He will be their strength. He will be their courage.

On the other side of the line I will invite to stand those political leaders who are self-satisfied, proud, haughty and arrogant, who think they know it all, who have deluded

---

[99] Daniel chapters 7-12

[100] Revelation chapters 1-22

[101] Matthew 24:42

themselves into believing that they can be like God, who have deceived themselves into thinking that they can live without God, who would rather die (and they will) than bow down, worship, and serve Him.

Every political leader must choose one of the two sides. There is no such thing as being neutral towards God; you're either with Him, or you're against Him. If you profess neutrality, you will be deemed to have made a choice to stand with those who stand against God.

Furthermore, there's no 51% commitment to being on God's side. There's no 80% or even 99% commitment. You're either all in, or you're not in at all.

THE CONSEQUENCES OF YOUR CHOICE

At the End of Days, after The Heavenly Warrior, which is Christ the Lord, defeats the Beast of the *Book of Revelations*, the first group of political leaders (those who stand with God) will be invited as honored guests to the Wedding Supper of the Lamb. [102]

The second group of political leaders (those who stand against God, including those who profess neutrality) will be invited to BE the main course at the supper of the birds:

> *And I saw an angel standing in the sun, who*
> *cried in a loud voice to all the birds flying in*
> *midair, "Come, gather together for the great*
> *supper of God, so that you may eat the flesh of*
> *kings, generals, and the mighty, of horses and*
> *their riders, and the flesh of all people, free and*
> *slave, great and small."*
> *Then I saw the beast and the kings of the earth*
> *and their armies gathered together to wage war*
> *against the rider on the horse and his army. But*

---

[102] Revelation 19:7-10

*the beast was captured, and with it the false
prophet who had performed the signs on its
behalf. With these signs he had deluded those
who had received the mark of the beast and
worshiped its image. The two of them were
thrown alive into the fiery lake of burning
sulfur. The rest were killed with the sword
coming out of the mouth of the rider on the
horse, and all the birds gorged themselves on
their flesh.* [103]

I won't apologize for being so blunt, so graphic, for I would do you no favors if I sugar-coated the choice you have to make. It's literally a matter of life-and-death for you, both in the here-and-now and in the hereafter. And if you're thinking that your suffering may be short-lived if you choose wrong, consider that you may spend eternity with Satan himself:

*And the devil, who deceived them, was thrown
into the lake of burning sulfur, where the beast
and the false prophet had been thrown. They
will be tormented day and night for ever and
ever.* [104]

ON CHOOSING SIDES

As we move into the Final Act of History, all the sides you've ever imagined as being important are no longer important – if they ever were at all.

There's no American side, no Russian side, no Chinese side, or any other side that has anything to do with any nation.

---

[103] Revelation 19:17-21

[104] Revelation 20:10

There's no communist side, no anti-communist side, no fascist side, no anti-fascist side, no conservative side, no Tea Party side, no liberal side, no progressive side, no libertarian side, no pro-environmental side, or any other side that has anything to do with political ideology.

There's no Catholic side, no Evangelical side, no Mainline Protestant side, no Mormon side, no Jewish side, no Shi'ite or Sunni Muslim side, no Buddhist side, no Hindu side, or any other side that has anything to do with religion.

There are no sides that matter that have anything to do with class, race, gender, sexual orientation, or anything else that mankind seems to keep themselves worked up about.

There are now, and always have been, only two sides that truly matter: you're either on God's side, or you're against Him. There's not even a neutral side.

> *Now when Joshua was near Jericho, he looked up and saw a man standing in front of him with a drawn sword in his hand. Joshua went up to him and asked, "Are you for us or for our enemies?"*
>
> *"Neither," he replied, "but as commander of the army of the Lord I have now come." Then Joshua fell facedown to the ground in reverence...* [105]

Whether in war or any other human activity, God doesn't take sides. He IS a side, the only side that matters, the only side that will still be standing at the End of History.

---

[105] Joshua 5:13-14

A Time To Choose

So now it's time for you to choose. Consider carefully your answers to the questions which follow. I will not assign you a side based on your answers. The Sovereign God will examine your heart and mind and He will know on which side you have already chosen to stand:

> *"The heart is hopelessly dark and deceitful,*
> *a puzzle that no one can figure out.*
> *But I, God, search the heart*
> *and examine the mind.*
> *I get to the heart of the human.*
> *I get to the root of things.*
> *I treat them as they really are,*
> *not as they pretend to be."* [106]

The Sovereign God Asks These Questions of All Political Leaders of Earth

---

1. *Who do you love more? Yourself, or the Sovereign God?*

2. *Which do you love more? The power, prestige, and privilege of your political position, or the Sovereign God?*

3. *When you look into the faces of the governed do you see sheep to be manipulated, or do you see the reflection of the Sovereign God in whose image they were made?*

4. *Which do you prefer? To serve your own interests and ambitions, or to serve the Sovereign God?*

---

[106] Jeremiah 17:10 (MSG)

6. *Would you rather dwell in the tents of the wicked for ten thousand days, or be a doorkeeper for one day in the House of God?* [107]

7. *Do you believe you're entitled to special rights and privileges as a result of your political position, or do you have the same mindset as Christ Jesus, "who, being in very nature God, did not consider equality with God something to be used to his own advantage; rather, he made himself nothing by taking the very nature of a servant?"* [108]

8. *Who is your master? The elites, the powerbrokers, the moneyed interests, the corporations, the unions, the political parties, on whom you think your power and position depend, or the Sovereign God on whom your life depends?*

9. *Would you prefer to champion the cause of the powerful, the strong, the rich, or to champion the cause of the powerless, the weak, the needy?*

10. *Will you tolerate injustice, oppression and corruption, or will you stand with the Sovereign God against them?*

11. *Will you stand before the Sovereign God ramrod straight, head held high, feet apart in a stance of pride and defiance, or will you bow down before Him in humility and reverential submission?*

* * * * * * * * * *

---

[107] Psalm 84:10

[108] Philippians 2:5-7

If there's good news here for those who choose foolishly on which side of the line they will stand, it's this: *"The Lord our God is merciful and forgiving, even though we have rebelled against him."* [109]

He may yet let you change your heart and mind right up until the moment it's too late. The trick, if you can call it that, is knowing the last moment just before the moment when it's too late to change. No one has yet mastered that trick and you're not likely to master it either.

---

[109] Daniel 9:9

CHAPTER 10

A MESSAGE TO THE NATIONS: "COME HOME!"

*What Satan put into the heads of our remote
ancestors was the idea that they could "be like
gods" –could set up on their own as if they had
created themselves – be their own masters –
invent some sort of happiness for themselves
outside God, apart from God. And out of that
hopeless attempt has come nearly all that we
call human history – money, poverty, ambition,
war, prostitution, classes, empires, slavery – the
long terrible story of man trying to find
something other than God which will make him
happy.*

*God cannot give us a happiness and peace apart
from Himself, because it is not there. There is
no such thing.* [110]

GOD OF JUDGMENT AND OF MERCY

As the curtain rises on the Final Act of the Human
Drama the Hand of the Lord is upon me. As the Day of
Reckoning, the Day of Judgment, approaches, He does not
want anyone to perish, but wants everyone to come to
repentance. [111]

---

[110] C.S. Lewis, *Mere Christianity (New York: Macmillan, 1952), pp 53-54*

[111] 2 Peter 3:9

The Sovereign God has directed me to say to you the words He spoke to Israel through the prophet Ezekiel some 2600 years ago:

> *'As surely as I live, declares the Sovereign Lord,*
> *I take no pleasure in the death of the wicked,*
> *but rather that they turn from their ways and*
> *live. Turn! Turn from your evil ways! Why will*
> *you die ...?'* [112]

The Sovereign God pleads with you to turn from *your* ways and to turn towards *His Ways.* You have strayed far from where you belong and He wants you to come home.

The Sovereign God sends me to personally deliver an urgent message to the nations, and to all the men, women and children who inhabit them:

> *Come to your senses! Come home before the*
> *road home becomes impassible and you are cut*
> *off from Me forever. Come home and I will give*
> *you shelter. I will comfort you and protect you*
> *during the difficult days that lie ahead.*

The Sovereign God declares that there is a moral and spiritual famine in the land and that it is global, affecting every nation; affecting every man, woman and child therein.

The Spirit of the Lord prompts me to re-interpret a parable told by Jesus to His disciples, but with a different emphasis to which you may not be accustomed, but which will soon sound familiar. It applies both to the nations and to all citizens of earth.

---

[112] Ezekiel 33:11

The Parable of the Lost Son [113]

It's sometimes called the Parable of the Prodigal Son, placing the emphasis on how the son squandered his inheritance on a wasteful and extravagant lifestyle. It's more appropriate here to refer to it as the Parable of the Lost Son, placing the emphasis on the consequences of the son having separated himself from his father.

A man had two sons, though they could just as easily be daughters today. One son was obedient, believing his father knew best, so he did whatever his father asked him to do. The disobedient son chafed under the direct rule of his father, even though his father was kind, loving and generous.

The disobedient son wanted to be known as his own man, not as his father's son. He wasn't so sure that his father knew best; he wanted to substitute his own judgment for that of his father. He wasn't willing to take his father's word for what was "true" or "right"; he wanted to decide for himself what was "true" and "right" for him.

The disobedient son no longer wanted to live under his father's roof where he'd have to live by his father's rules; he wanted to make up and live by his own rules. He didn't want to be accountable to anybody, especially his father. He wanted to find out what pleasures his father was keeping from him by keeping him down on the farm.

The story echoes of the original sin of Adam and Eve which led to the Fall of Man. For just as they aspired to "*be like God*," the disobedient son longed to substitute himself for his father, to step into his father's shoes, and to chart his own course in life.

So the disobedient son exercised his legal right to demand his inheritance (one-half of his father's estate) so that he could set out on his own. He left the farm and went into the big city, where he proceeded to explore every way

---

[113] Luke 15:11-32

imaginable to recklessly and sinfully spend every last penny of his inheritance.

After a while, the disobedient son had absolutely nothing left: no money, no friends, not even a shred of dignity. He was reduced to finding any type of work he could get and ended up feeding pigs – an animal that was considered unclean in his culture. He was so hungry that he eventually got down on his hands and knees in the mud and the filth of the pig pen and competed with the pigs for any and every scrap of food he could wrestle away from them.

When he had fallen as low as any man could go, he finally came to his senses and said "*How many of my father's hired servants have food to spare, and here I am starving to death!*" [114] He resolved to go home, confess his errors, beg for his father's forgiveness, and offer to work as one of his father's hired servants, just so he could have a roof over his head and decent food to eat.

Most tellers of the story would proceed to what is commonly thought to be the main point: "*while he was still a long way off, his father saw him and was filled with compassion for him; he ran to his son, threw his arms around him and kissed him.*" [115] The disobedient son began the apology he'd been practicing for days, but he didn't get too far into it when

> *... the father said to his servants, 'Quick! Bring the best robe and put it on him. Put a ring on his finger and sandals on his feet. Bring the fattened calf and kill it. Let's have a feast and celebrate. For this son of mine was dead and is alive again; he was lost and is found.' So they began to celebrate.* [116]

---

[114] Luke 15:17

[115] Luke 15:20

[116] Luke 15:22-24

This post-pig-pen part of the story is a wonderful, happy ending that shifts the focus from the wanton acts of the disobedient son to the attributes of the loving, generous, forgiving father. This is a good thing, for it brings the story full circle, and it's an accurate depiction of your Heavenly Father.

But the Sovereign God wants you to go back to that pig pen and focus on the moment of truth – that precarious moment when the disobedient son's future, his very life, hung in the balance. The son had done everything his own way rather than his father's way. His decisions had brought him to ruin and to the brink of starvation. And now he had to make what could be the most important decision of his entire life.

WHAT IF HE HAD NOT COME TO HIS SENSES?

If the disobedient son had not come to his senses, if he had not decided to turn back and return to his father's home, he would have died there in that pig pen. He had lost his way. He was lost to himself. And he would have been lost to his father forever.

The Sovereign God IS that father. And you are that disobedient son, or daughter. He is watching the road every day, scanning the horizon for any sign of you. He is waiting for you to come home. He longs for you to come home. He has even sent me as His Messenger to plead with you:

> *Return ... to the Lord your God.*
> *Your sins have been your downfall!* [117]

If you return home now, He will embrace you. He will clothe you in the best robe. He will put sandals on your bare, bruised, and bleeding feet. He will put a ring on your finger.

---

[117] Hosea 14:1

He will have the fattened calf killed and all of heaven will come to rejoice at your welcome home party. You once were dead and are alive again; you were lost to Him and now are found. Your return home will be a cause for great celebration, for *"there will be more rejoicing in heaven over one sinner who repents than over ninety-nine righteous persons who do not need to repent."* [118]

And Yet, You will Not Be Willing

"*God so loved the world that he gave his one and only Son, that whoever believes in him shall not perish but have eternal life.*" [119] Just days before He was to be crucified Jesus wept over Jerusalem. [120] He did not weep for Himself in anticipation of the events to come, but for the inhabitants of Jerusalem:

> *"Jerusalem, Jerusalem, you who kill the prophets and stone those sent to you, how often I have longed to gather your children together, as a hen gathers her chicks under her wings, and you were not willing.* [121]

- He wept over them because they would not come to their senses and come home.
- He weeps for you now because He knows that many who hear this message will ignore it.
- He weeps for you now because He knows that many of you will not come to your senses.

---

[118] Luke 15:7

[119] John 3:16

[120] John 11:35

[121] Matthew 23:37

- He weeps for you now because He knows that many of you will continue to wallow in the mud and filth of your sin.
- He weeps for you now because He knows that many of you will die face down in the mud and filth of that pig pen.
- He weeps for you now because He knows that many of you are not coming home.
- He weeps for you now because He knows there will be no welcome home party, for you will be lost to Him forever.

As the one who's sacred duty it has been to deliver the Sovereign God's urgent plea to you to come to your senses and come home, I weep with the prophet Jeremiah:

> *Oh, that my head were a spring of water*
> *and my eyes a fountain of tears!*
> *I would weep day and night*
> *for the slain of my people.* [122]

The Spirit of the Lord is upon me. I plead with you one last time:

Come to your senses!

Come home!

---

[122] Jeremiah 9:1

AFTERWORD

HOW YOU CAN HELP TO RELEASE GOD'S POWER

And the Lord said to me, "Write my answer on a billboard, large and clear, so that anyone can read it at a glance and rush to tell the others."
[123]

"This is what the Lord says to you: 'Do not be afraid or discouraged because of this vast army. For the battle is not yours, but God's.'" [124]

THE CURTAIN IS RISING; THE "ENDGAME" HAS BEGUN

The curtain is already rising on the Final Act of the Human Drama. The "endgame" of history has begun. The timing, the details of what will happen, and the sequence of events are unknown to all but the Sovereign God. While we cannot prove these things to the satisfaction of the skeptics, we know these things by faith, which is "the assurance of things hoped for, the conviction of things not seen. [125] But here is what we do know.

While we cannot know the day, the hour, or the minute of its arrival, we know that the Day of Reckoning, the Day of Judgment, *is* imminent.

---

[123] Habakkuk 2:2 (TLB)

[124] 2 Chronicles 20: 15

[125] Hebrews 11:1

While we cannot know the day, the hour, or the minute of His Coming, we know that the Lord Jesus *will* return in triumph.

While we cannot know the day, the hour, or the minute that the Kingdom of God will arrive, arrive it will and we can all agree that it won't be one minute too soon!

While we cannot know the day, the hour, or the minute of his downfall, the Lord Jesus has already told us that He has seen the moment when "*Satan [will] fall like lightning from heaven*" [126] – namely he will fall from the skies when the full power of heaven is brought to bear upon him.

While we cannot know how the specifics of the "end time" battles will play out, or be certain of which nations will stand with God and which will stand against Him, we do know for a certainty that the Sovereign God will be victorious and that Satan, death, destruction, and chaos (unleashed by the rebellion of Adam and Eve) will be defeated once and for all.

FAITH IS OUR CONCERN; OUTCOMES ARE GOD'S CONCERN

The "endgame" is God's to plan and to fulfill. While I'll get to how you can help to release God's power in a moment, it's important to make clear that this is the Lord's battle not ours.

In my previous book, *Our Eyes Are On You: Building Rock-Solid Faith for Faith-Shaking Times*, [127] I told the story of a massive army bearing down on Jerusalem when Jehoshaphat was king. [128] "*Alarmed, Jehoshaphat resolved to inquire of the Lord, and he proclaimed a fast for all Judah.*" [129] Citizens from all over Judah gathered in the public square

---

[126] Luke 10:18

[127] Currently out of print, but a new edition will be coming in early 2015

[128] 2 Chronicles 20:1-30

[129] 2 Chronicles 20:3

of Jerusalem and sought the Lord's help. Jehoshaphat ended his prayer with words that should be stored up in your heart and seared into your memory:

> *"[W]e have no power to face this vast army that is attacking us. We do not know what to do, but our eyes are on you.".* [130]

At the conclusion of Jehoshaphat's prayer, all the men, women and children, stayed put, waiting for, expecting a response from God. They didn't have to wait long. The Spirit fell upon a man in the crowd who stood up and said:

> *"Listen, King Jehoshaphat and all who live in Judah and Jerusalem! This is what the Lord says to you: 'Do not be afraid or discouraged because of this vast army. For the battle is not yours, but God's. Tomorrow march down against them. … You will not have to fight this battle. Take up your positions; stand firm and see the deliverance the Lord will give you, Judah and Jerusalem. Do not be afraid; do not be discouraged. Go out to face them tomorrow, and the Lord will be with you.'"* [131]

The people praised God, went home and got a good night's rest. The next morning they gathered again, suited up for battle, even though they didn't know how the battle was going to play out. Jehoshaphat reminded them of the promise of God. The people praised God some more, then marched off towards the place where the enemy armies were to be found, singing and praising God all the way. And when they arrived, God set ambushes and caused all of the enemy

---

[130] 2 Chronicles 20:12

[131] 2 Chronicles 20:15-17

armies to kill each other. At the site of God's Great Victory, the people of Judah praised Him some more. They never had to swing a sword, throw a spear, or deflect an enemy blow. God had fought their battle for them, and had won. And they went back to Jerusalem and praised God some more.

In the battles which are to come during the End of Days, we must have that same steady faith. We must take up our positions. We must not be afraid. We must stand firm in our faith. And then we simply watch what God is doing, and will do, to deliver us.

YOUR TO DO LIST:
PRAY

The number one way to release God's power in the world is to pray: *"The prayer of a righteous person is powerful and effective."* [132]

Praise God for his faithfulness throughout history and praise Him for his faithfulness now, especially in your own life.

Pray that the faithful of every nation will be strengthened to take up their positions, to not be afraid, to stand firm, and to watch what God is doing, and is about to do, for them and in the world.

Pray that God will uproot all wicked political leaders around the world, and replace them with God-fearing, effective, and virtuous political leaders.

Pray that the political leaders of your nation, your state or province, your region, your city or town, will choose to stand *with* God rather than against Him.

Pray that all those who have strayed from God will come to their senses and come home to God, before it is too late, before the road home becomes impassible, and they are cut off forever. This is not a time to be bashful but to be bold.

---

[132] James 5:16

Name names. Pray specifically for people you know and love (whether they be family, friends, or acquaintances) if you believe they have strayed from God, need to come to their senses, and come home to Him.

And for me, God's Messenger:

- Pray that I may declare the Sovereign God's Message fearlessly. [133]
- Pray that I may extend His invitation mercifully.
- Pray that I may declare His warning boldly.
- Pray that my voice will convey tenderness when delivering a message of mercy.
- Pray that my voice will convey rolling thunder when delivering a message of warning and of judgment.

YOUR TO DO LIST: SPREAD THE WORD

The Sovereign God said to Habakkuk: *"Write my answer on a billboard, large and clear, so that anyone can read it at a glance and rush to tell the others."* [134]

In the spirit of Habakkuk, I've delivered the Word of God as faithfully, as boldly, and as clearly as I know how. The Sovereign God has told me to keep this book short so that you can "read it at a glance." Now, if you embrace the message, rush to tell others.

Use social media. Use email. Send letters and postcards. Make phone calls. Strike up a conversation.

Buy the book for your friends and for your pastor. Buy a copy for your favorite (or least favorite) political leader and send it to him or her.

---

[133] Ephesians 6:20

[134] Habakkuk 2:2 (TLB)

But whatever you do, if you embrace the message, don't bottle it up in your heart where others who need to hear it will never hear it. Share the message so that others might be saved – both in the here-and-now and in the hereafter.

YOUR TO DO LIST: PUT ON THE FULL ARMOR OF GOD

We're not engaged in a political or ideological struggle, or a struggle between "good guys" and "bad guys".

> *Our struggle is not against flesh and blood, but against the rulers, against the authorities, against the powers of this dark world and against the spiritual forces of evil in the heavenly realms.* [135]

You've heard it said: "Don't bring a knife to a gun fight." This is not a battle where you show up in your beach shorts, tee-shirt, and tennis shoes. This is serious business.

> *Put on the full armor of God, so that when the day of evil comes, you may be able to stand your ground, and after you have done everything, to stand.* [136]

What is the armor of God?

- *"the belt of truth buckled around your waist,"* [137]

- *"the breastplate of righteousness in place,"* [138]

---

[135] Ephesians 6:12

[136] Ephesians 6:13

[137] Ephesians 6:14

- *"your feet fitted with the readiness that comes from the gospel of peace;"* [139]

- *"the shield of faith, with which you can extinguish all the flaming arrows of the evil one;"* [140]

- *"the helmet of salvation;"* [141] and

- *"the sword of the Spirit, which is the word of God."* [142]

A FINAL WORD OF HOPE

Keep your eyes fixed on God!

Be watching for the Lord's coming!

Be listening for the hoof beats of the Heavenly Cavalry!

Stand firm in your faith!

Have courage!

Watch!

---

[138] Ephesians 6:14

[139] Ephesians 6:15

[140] Ephesians 6:16

[141] Ephesians 6:17

[142] Ephesians 6:17

* * * * * * * * * *

"The Lord bless you
and keep you;

the Lord make his face shine on you
and be gracious to you;

the Lord turn his face toward you
and give you peace." [143]

---

[143] Numbers 6:24-26

ABOUT THE AUTHOR

Speaker and author R. ALAN SMITH has a Juris Doctor degree from the University of San Diego School of Law and a Bachelor of Art's degree (Sociology major / Business minor) from Graceland University. He is also a Registered Corporate Coach™ and Affiliate Member of the Worldwide Association of Business Coaches. With expertise in building and sustaining momentum for ideas, initiatives and the future, Smith has had a diverse career: lawyer, political professional, nonprofit association executive, governmental affairs professional, strategic advisor, executive coach, and university professor. In addition to *Every Knee Shall Bow*, he has at least ten more books in various stages of development, including a new edition of a previous book, *Our Eyes Are On You: Building Rock-Solid Faith for Faith-Shaking Times* (new edition coming in first quarter of 2015). A resident of San Diego, California for much of the past forty years, Smith has three passions in life: (1) serving God in whatever manner God directs; (2) loving his family; and (3) developing effective and virtuous political leaders around the world.

Speaker/Author Website:

www.ralansmith.net

READER'S NOTES

READER'S NOTES

READER'S NOTES

READER'S NOTES

READER'S NOTES

READER'S NOTES

READER'S NOTES

READER'S NOTES